Wholehearted Love is a powerful and r[...]
will leave you with a full heart and a f[...]
Stefanie have masterfully interwoven biblical truth and practical
principles with the narrative of their own epic, real-life love story.
Whether you are single, dating, engaged, or married, this book
will remind you of God's perfect plan for your life and your
relationships.

DAVE AND ASHLEY WILLIS
Bestselling authors and hosts of *The Naked Marriage* podcast

Wholehearted Love is a deeply moving exploration of love in all its
complexities and nuances. Caleb and Stefanie capture the essence of
human connection, delving into the depths of passion, heartbreak,
and the transformative power of love. With its raw emotional
depth, this extraordinary book will resonate with readers, reminding
them of the profound beauty and challenges common to the
universal experience of love.

ANDREW F. CARTER
Lead pastor of Royal City Church, author, and speaker

Just the idea of loving without abandon can be intimidating, but
Stefanie and Caleb bring so much hope for each one of us on every
page of *Wholehearted Love*. Not only are they incredible people,
but they really love and care for others, and it shows in this book.
I cannot recommend this enough for anyone who desires to love
wholeheartedly.

LEANNA CRAWFORD
CCM songwriter/artist

Caleb and Stefanie's book is a profound and transformative guide
for anyone yearning to cultivate healthy love relationships. With
grace and vulnerability, they address the areas of the heart that can
be unhealthy and toxic, and they offer practical steps toward finding
healing and restoration. The "Making It Personal" sections at the
end of each chapter allow readers to embark on a personal journey

of self-discovery, making this book an essential tool for those seeking healing and growth in their relationships.

MIKE SIGNORELLI
Lead pastor, V1 Church

I am so thankful Stefanie and Caleb wrote this book! It identifies real areas of struggle we deal with privately and quietly, and it helps us feel less alone and more equipped. Wholehearted love is the ultimate goal, but there are so many blocks that can prevent us from having what we were made for. After this read, you'll be able to take hold of the love God died to give you.

KRISTEN DALTON WOLFE
Author of *The Sparkle Effect*, success and fulfillment coach, Miss USA 2009

Wholehearted Love is a tribute to the transcendent love we have in our heavenly Father and an empowerment to mirror it in our earthly relationships. This book equips readers with the tools and insights needed to overcome the obstacles that can hinder relationships, and it allows them to transform their thinking and create lasting impact.

ARDEN AND CHRISTIAN BEVERE
Authors and podcast hosts

This book is a rare gift because it takes the dislocation of pain and disappointment seriously while offering us pathways to peace and wholeness. Authentic, practical, and accessible—there's something here for everyone who's seeking to know and be known. Well done, Caleb and Stefanie!

ADDISON BEVERE
Messenger International, author of *Words with God*

Stefanie and Caleb have chosen to lean into the pain associated with the tribulation promised to each person, and God has used them tremendously. Vulnerability is the gateway to connectivity, and this power couple has taken what could have destroyed them and turned it into an incredible ministry.

JOSHUA BROOME
Speaker and author

Wholehearted Love is a wonderful book, full of engaging stories and wisdom. It gives practical steps to experience deeper freedom in your thoughts and your personal life!

JENESSA WAIT
Artist and author

God has raised Stefanie and Caleb Rouse to be a voice to their generation. . . . Nothing impacts our daily lives more than the health of our intimate relationships. This book provides a clear path to both identifying and overcoming the barriers to that health while providing a way forward so we can experience God's grace and peace in our relationships. Dig into this book and begin to live your best relational life!

JOHN NUZZO
Lead pastor, Victory Family Church

Caleb and Stefanie have been integral in my life and path—talk about "the real deal" kind of people. I genuinely don't know where I would be without their grace-filled guidance and family heart toward me—they are a sliver of heaven. I have no doubt *Wholehearted Love* will bless, encourage, and impact your life in ways that'll last a lifetime!

COLLIN LABROSSE, @COLLINLABROSSE
Social media influencer and MMA fighter

Wholehearted Love is packed with profound revelations that will reshape the way you view relationships and bring extraordinary healing to your heart. With grace as their compass, Caleb and Stefanie navigate the complexities of unhealthy love and toxic patterns with wisdom, unfiltered vulnerability, and gentle guidance.

Their words resonate deeply, offering practical steps toward restoration and renewal through the timeless truths of Scripture. This book is a powerful testament to the beauty that awaits when we surrender to God's perfect plan for love, illuminating a path toward a life lived authentically, wholeheartedly, and abundantly.

CHAD AND TORI MASTERS
Faith-based YouTubers and hosts of *Mornings with the Masters* daily devotional podcast

What a unique gift this book is to those who may have lost hope in love. Our friends Caleb and Stefanie share ashes-to-beauty stories that tug at your heart . . . and you will certainly find part of your story in theirs. This book helps the brokenhearted to hel and speaks truth and hope into broken places. *Wholehearted Love* is their authentic way of guiding you through the pain of your past and leading you to the healthy life God intends for you!

MONTELL AND KRISTIN JORDAN
Pastors, authors, and friends

Wholehearted Love is an absolute must-read if you want to feel inspired and awestruck by the goodness and faithfulness of God. The vulnerable storytelling in this book makes the reader feel as though they are walking with Stefanie and Caleb through their incredible story, which was written by God and is a true testimony of God's love to all who read.

JACOB AND JULIA PETERSEN
Social media content creators

I dearly love Caleb and Stefanie Rouse. They are helping people find true love and build their dream marriage. In their new book, *Wholehearted Love*, you will be captivated by their stories and learn how to grow deeper in love with your spouse or, if you are not married yet, how to find and pursue true love.

MATT BROWN
Evangelist; author of *Truth Plus Love*; founder of Think Eternity

Wholehearted Love

STEFANIE & CALEB ROUSE

wholehearted
LOVE

OVERCOME THE BARRIERS THAT HOLD YOU BACK
IN YOUR RELATIONSHIP WITH GOD AND OTHERS
AND DELIGHT IN FEELING SAFE, SEEN, AND LOVED

TYNDALE
MOMENTUM®

A Tyndale nonfiction imprint

Visit Tyndale online at tyndale.com.

Visit Tyndale Momentum online at tyndalemomentum.com.

Visit Stefanie and Caleb online at stefanieandcaleb.com.

Tyndale, Tyndale's quill logo, *Tyndale Momentum*, and the Tyndale Momentum logo are registered trademarks of Tyndale House Ministries. Tyndale Momentum is a nonfiction imprint of Tyndale House Publishers, Carol Stream, Illinois.

Designed by Julie Chen

Edited by Donna L. Berg

Published in association with The Bindery Agency, www.TheBinderyAgency.com.

For information about special discounts for bulk purchases, please contact Tyndale House Publishers at csresponse@tyndale.com, or call 1-855-277-9400.

Library of Congress Cataloging-in-Publication Data

A catalog record for this book is available from the Library of Congress.

ISBN 978-1-4964-7401-8

Printed in the United States of America

30	29	28	27	26	25	24
7	6	5	4	3	2	1

To our sweet twin boys, Asher and Shiloh,
we wish you were here with us.
Thank you for showing us a whole new way to love.
You both are such a gift, and we can't wait to
hug and kiss you one day in heaven.
This book is for you.

And to you, the one holding this book
and reading these words,
God sees you.
We pray this book will ignite dreams
once dead in your heart and bring hope
and light to even the darkest places.

Contents

Foreword

GROWING UP IN a small Midwestern town, I (Chelsea) didn't have many options for a vibrant, loving dating relationship. There were more cornfields than the eye could see, and farming families named their streets after their last name. I couldn't see a future with any of the guys around (I'd surveyed the land). I don't think I was extremely picky, but I like to believe I just knew what I wanted. After a couple of lonely years, I decided to date the guys I *didn't* see a future with because I thought they were all that was out there. *Surely, I just have to settle because these are my only option?* I thought.

This was the common theme I saw when I was growing up: date in middle school and high school, then somewhere in college or after college, get married. Most people married their high school sweethearts. But from afar, I saw a lot of settling. Like me, others thought that if they settled and got married, their relationship would naturally improve just because they took it to the next step of engagement or marriage.

Just for a second, imagine you broke a bone. Ouch. The healing process afterward is anything but fast. Healing requires you to slow down, possibly be on crutches, and live a little differently for a period. If you don't, you'll walk around with a wound that only gets worse and can lead other parts of the body to get damaged too.

Many couples walk into their love lives like they are on crutches, with open wounds that have never healed. They didn't take the time to heal from the past (rejection, pain, or cheating), and this leads to further fear in the future—and sometimes even leads to self-sabotaging a good relationship!

Maybe you've struggled with swirling thoughts about your own relationships because of what you've seen in relationships close to you: divorce, infidelity, or addiction.

Questions and thoughts like these may have surfaced for you:

Am I even capable of a loving, committed relationship?

I've seen far too many relationships fail—what if I'm just part of the divorce statistic?

My parents divorced—I could end up just like them.

I've been treated like trash in past relationships. What can turn that around?

Is there something wrong with me that I attract people who continually hurt me?

The list goes on.

As we were reading *Wholehearted Love*, we felt ourselves being deeply counseled and given tools that we can implement in our marriage. And what a blessing this book would have been before marriage or when we were dating! With each chapter, Stefanie and Caleb pull back the layers of a beautiful onion (as Shrek would say) and get to the root of some challenges that could be holding you back from a flourishing relationship. If you are open to healing, you will receive it!

We are sure this book will leave you way better than before—and more empowered to live and love wholeheartedly. We pray you will live in the fullness of what your relationship could be!

Chelsea and Nick Hurst
Speakers, online communicators, and authors

Prologue

"Happy Valen-time's Day, Mommy!" I shouted as I ran down the steps to make the school bus. I threw my arms around her in a big hug.

"Happy Valentine's Day, sweetie! I hope you have the best day." She loved the way I pronounced Valen-times and thought it was sweet how intentional I was in thinking of others on all the special holidays.

She handed me my pink, yellow, and blue backpack, which matched my outfit, and I was giddy with excitement over the precious cargo inside: Little Mermaid and Beauty and the Beast cards addressed to my classmates, with lollipops attached to each one. I couldn't wait to show my friends how much I cared about them, and I had written a special card to a boy I liked. I wondered how many cards and treats I would get in return. And would that boy give *me* a special card too?

Valentine's Day for me was filled with anticipation. It was a time to show others I cared. I loved getting candy, and I loved hearing nice words from others, and I loved telling others nice things. It seemed like the best kind of day.

My childlike joy for this holiday stayed over the years. Although I stopped giving out Little Mermaid cards, I still found cute ways to celebrate. Fast-forward to the year I was going to graduate from college. This next Valentine's Day was bound to be the best one yet . . .

Over Christmas break, my boyfriend Todd had popped the question with a gorgeous diamond ring and an elaborate *Pretty Woman* theme. I was happy but kept feeling like something wasn't right.

I hadn't spent much time at home the last several years, other than for Christmas and spring breaks. I had an apartment at Penn State, where I was attending school, and I was volunteering twenty hours a week in a high school ministry. In the summers, I worked near campus. My family was three hours away, and because I was so busy, I didn't find much time to go back home. But in those rare visits, sleeping in my childhood bed brought back many emotions.

The room was still decorated much like it was when I was a little girl. Pink flowers on the comforter, a pile of stuffed animals, some old band posters. Album after album filled with pictures of my friends and family. And a little white desk where I would sit for hours in my younger days, doing my makeup and writing letters to my friends and boyfriends. That Christmas, I opened the drawer and started reading through some old notes. I reminisced about the silly things my girlfriends and I would pen back and forth to each other—the boys we liked, what they said to us, how we were so glad to be friends.

And I pulled out my old journals. I gathered them in my arms and sat crisscross-applesauce on the bed. I had written almost daily since I learned to make full sentences, ending each entry with the words "I love you God, I love you Jesus, I love you Holy Spirit, I love my family, I love everyone in the world. God bless them all!"

As I flipped through the pages, I found an entry entitled "My Dream Man." It was a list of characteristics I longed to have in a future husband, penned in early high school.

Handsome
Loves God
Tall
Funny
Last name that starts with an S
Family lives close to my family
Good family
Has lots of money . . .

The list went on, but I called my mom into the room.

"Mom, you gotta check this out!" I exclaimed. "I can't believe I'm getting everything I've ever wished for. Todd has it all!"

"Wow, yes, that's pretty incredible." She appeared excited, but I noticed some hesitation in her voice. I felt in my gut like something was off with my relationship with my fiancé—that even though I was getting everything on my list, something big was missing. But I pushed the feelings down and picked up a bridal magazine to find my perfect dress.

Day after day the gut feeling kept creeping back. I brought up these concerns to Todd several times.

"I feel like something is not right," I said. "I feel rushed, and I can't shake this weird feeling. I think we should push back the wedding."

Todd kept assuring me that everything was fine. I was overthinking things, and it was my family's fault that I was feeling this way. We would stop having them in our life soon, and then I would feel better. Although this made me sad—I loved my family very much and it killed me to think of not being close to them anymore—I decided he probably knew best because he was older than me and way closer to God.

I distracted myself with wedding planning through break and into the New Year, and January was full of ministry and friends. Since Todd led the ministry I volunteered with and the meetings were held at his house, I couldn't wait to show my ring to all my friends, invite some of them to be bridesmaids, and tell them the whole proposal story. We purchased the bridesmaids' dresses, and I found the wedding gown I had always dreamed of. Todd and I chose our venue, caterer, DJ, and flowers. I loved the attention and special fellowship we all were sharing. The two of us felt loved and cared for by our community, and almost everyone was full of joy over our upcoming union, which was planned for May. My family supported the wedding financially and helped with some of the planning, although I kept sensing their hesitation.

I couldn't wait for Valentine's Day. The holiday I had loved since childhood was bound to be better than I could imagine—my first one as a woman engaged to be married!

When the day finally came, Todd had made a reservation at a nice local restaurant near Penn State. When he picked me up, I got in the car myself. In the early stages of dating, he would open the door for me, but not today. He handed me a yellow orchid with "Happy ValenTIMES Day" written on the container. I still pronounced the word wrong, and he loved letting me know that. Some of his comments had made me feel small over the course of our one-year relationship, but I tried to see it as all in good fun. I handed him a card about being excited to marry him and happy he was my fiancé.

During the car ride, I sat awkwardly, asking him several questions in an attempt to get a conversation going. He gave me only one-word answers. I thought he must have a lot on his mind, so I focused on my growling stomach—I was excited for some good food. I stared down at my hands, where my ring sparkled in the last glimmers of daylight. It was so beautiful, but my heart was heavy.

As we entered the restaurant, Todd gave the hostess his name and asked how she was with a kind smile. I hadn't gotten that smile so far that day. He talked to that stranger more than he had talked to me. She led us to the middle of the dimly lit restaurant, and we took our seats. I thanked Todd for the orchid and asked him how he was doing. "Fine," he said without even glancing up.

I stared at my menu. Being there was becoming painful. I ordered my meal but had a pit in my stomach when the food arrived. I tried to ask him several more questions, but he looked around the restaurant, as if he hadn't noticed. It was so uncomfortable sitting there in silence, and I couldn't wait to leave. *This isn't what I thought this day was going to be like*, I thought to myself.

We drove back to his condo in darkness and silence. I couldn't wait to get out of the car and just about sprinted to his living room after we pulled into the driveway.

I sat on his couch as I was accustomed to doing, and he sat opposite me.

"I need the engagement ring back," he finally said.

"WHAT!" I shouted. "What are you talking about?"

"The wedding is off. I need the ring back."

I kept asking, "Why? Why?" and he just kept saying the same thing: "Give me back the ring. The wedding is off."

The wind was knocked out of me, and my heart dropped to my knees. I blanked out and barely remember handing back the ring and running out of the house. I honestly can't recall whether I ran home or whether he drove me.

The next week was and is a complete blur. All I can remember is sobbing uncontrollably into my pillow and not sleeping all night. I remember him stopping over one day to make it clear that it wasn't just the wedding that was off: our relationship was over for good. He gave me no explanation, no other information. He told me I was no longer welcome to attend the meetings at his house because it would be too difficult for him.

In a flash, I lost my dream of being a wife. I lost my dream wedding. I lost many of my friends (because he was their boss), and I lost hope.

1

What's Your Dream?

ENVISIONING YOUR GOALS TO ENSURE
FULFILLING RELATIONSHIPS

CALEB'S STORY: THE DARK FOREST OF DISAPPOINTMENT

I always dreamed of what true love might be like, and I knew it was something I wanted. My father enjoys a good love story, and many times as a family we would take in the sweet aroma of romance through our collection of the classics. I have seen my fair share of romantic comedies and epic love tales.

There is something captivating about extravagant and pursuant love, whether it's in the stories of Romeo and Juliet, Jasmine and Aladdin, Prince Charming and Snow White, or any number of others. Take your pick and you'll find suspense, true love's kiss, and a tale that takes your breath away.

In the summer, my family would take a two-week road trip, crossing the country from California to Missouri to visit my two sets of grandparents. My father's parents resided in a small German town with original brick buildings, beautiful wineries, and a few general stores filled with townsfolk who had known each other for a lifetime.

My grandparents had a large old brick house outside of town. I could feel the memories from a hundred years ago as I walked through the halls, where pictures of family members I never knew were mixed in with photos of all my aunts and uncles. My grandparents were not ones for flashy living nor any type of modernity. Even using the bathroom, which had a window in the door, was an experience.

In the kitchen and living room area sat their vintage box TV. After a day of playing outside, my brothers and I would sit on the couch and watch one of three options for entertainment before bed: the movie *Free Willy*, recordings of World Cup soccer games from 1994 (I mean, how can you resist that?), or the cult classic *The Princess Bride*. Let's just say it was an easy choice: we watched *The Princess Bride* every night for a week straight.

If you haven't seen this movie, you need to; it's a classic love tale with unique humor. It's one of my favorites. Every summer, I would watch how true love conquers all, and I don't want to spoil it for you, but I learned that wholehearted love comes only to those brave enough to walk a scary and vulnerable road, where all hope seems lost until love makes a way.

Later, as an adult, I longed for a love like this. I had seen a glimpse of it—I had parents who loved each other, oftentimes acting like kids as they pulled pranks, laughed together, built a family, and went after their dreams.

And I wanted something like that: a partner, a best friend, and someone who would take on this epic adventure of life with me.

Unfortunately, life isn't easy, and love is even worse at times. Broken dreams and a wounded heart sent me down a path where all hope seemed lost. I had lost a relationship I had been in for five years, while simultaneously losing out on my dream of being a professional athlete. Those two losses, along with the death of an important person in my life, led me to distrust God and His purpose for me. I went searching for love and hope in all the wrong places, and it left me feeling empty, alone, and scared for the future.

I felt many times like I was living in a deep forest, where I couldn't see above the trees. My future was dark and cloudy, and the path in front of me was bleak and barely visible.

I realized that something had to change, but what? And would it be worth fighting through the branches that had grown out of my pain, obstructing the path to change and leaving me resistant to even trying? Was it worth putting my heart out there again, with the possibility of more loss and disappointment just around the bend?

You might find yourself at a similar crossroads. Life hasn't been the easiest, and maybe you have been patiently waiting for your person for years, losing hope day by day, hour by hour, and minute by minute. You see the dream you have always wanted, but there are many unknowns.

Two paths lie in front of you. One is safe and shorter, and the likely outcome is similar to the situation you've been in. The other ends in the dreams you've always wanted, but the road is long and filled with unknowns, fears, and vulnerability.

Maybe you've found yourself right here in this book because you want that Prince Charming and Snow White kind of love. You always have. You just don't know if it is possible for you. And maybe it's made you distance yourself from God. Maybe you feel like you can't be fully yourself in a relationship.

I want you to know that I see you, friend.

Your pain isn't wasted. It is real. And at this crossroads I encourage you to take a long look at what you want. What your dream is.

What you have always wanted your life to look like and feel like. And decide, is it worth taking this new road?

STEFANIE'S STORY: FINDING HOME

But God.

I've found these to be two of my favorite words. I'm sure you have guessed that the story in the prologue is my story. After the heartbreak of that broken engagement, I didn't know if I would ever have another relationship or get married. But God came through in a way I had never experienced before.

I remember sitting on a park bench and telling Jesus, "I'd rather it just be You and me forever than to be back with all the things of this world without You." And I meant it. God's love without striving, trying to prove myself, or worrying about performance was better than anything I'd ever experienced. There was no going back.

And Jesus sent me on a quest. He showed me my true purpose and flipped everything I thought I knew about love and relationships upside right.

It put a fire in my soul that made me want to help so many others who have experienced the pain of heartbreak. Becoming exactly who Jesus created me to be and loving Him and the ones He's called me to love with my whole heart is a journey I've been on ever since.

I felt called to leave my home in Pennsylvania and make a cross-country move to Pasadena, California, where I would earn my master's degree in marriage and family therapy at Fuller Theological Seminary. Leaving was frightening, yet hopeful. I felt the still, small voice of the Lord in my heart, leading me away, wooing me to find my purpose and future.

After two years of completing hard coursework and fulfilling hours of counseling clients, I finally had done enough to receive my degree and begin work in therapy. Then one Sunday, a very tall, handsome man entered my life. As Caleb tells it, he saw me from across the room as we were worshiping in church, and it was love at first sight. How we began to date is a long story (one that we will share later in this book), but we eventually crossed paths again a year later. Caleb asked for my phone number, and we went on our first date. Our hearts had never connected with another person in such a powerful way before. We felt like we were home to each other. We knew we were safe, seen, and loved for who we were, and for the first time ever, we both felt like we could love wholeheartedly in a romantic relationship.

We got married just over a year after our first date and started working together at a Christian school in our area. Caleb's master's degree is in education, and he had been working in the school system for a few years prior. We embarked on a new career together, trying to make a positive impact on youth for Christ. I was given the opportunity to develop my own curriculum within the Bible department, creating lessons on relationships and family dynamics, which led to remarkable breakthroughs in my students' lives. After three years at the school, I felt a calling from the Lord to take this work online and start sharing about relationships and God's love through social media.

By the grace of God, this has brought opportunities that we never thought we would have—traveling the world, seeing new places, meeting people from all over, sharing about God's beautiful love. In all of these situations, we've assured others that wholehearted love is possible, as we have experienced it in our own marriage.

Eventually, Caleb was able to leave his job as a teacher to pursue this work full-time with me. Through this new venture we developed a program called Cultivate Relationship where single women and men can come to us and find freedom from their past and gain the tools needed to have successful and thriving relationships in the future. It is also a powerful course for newly engaged and married couples to set up their relationship for long-term success.[1]

Through our courses and programs we have been able to touch the lives of hundreds of people from around the world, helping them move past heartbreak and move toward wholehearted love. Now God has put it on our hearts to share this message with you. I'm so honored to join you for part of this journey throughout these pages.

WHOLEHEARTED LOVE CAN BE YOUR STORY TOO

Dear friend, you've read the beginnings of our story, and we'll share more about our own heartaches and triumphs in later chapters. You may find that your story is similar to ours. Perhaps the pain you've faced and the circumstances you've experienced have been too much to handle. There's no way to face that much anguish and not do something about it. Sometimes we put on a mask and armor to protect ourselves from further injury. The burden of the mask is so heavy, but it's more desirable than feeling vulnerable and unsafe.

God knows that this life can be hard. He knows the troubles we will face. And He wants us to exchange the masks and armor we've created for the most powerful armor of all.

We wish we could talk to you in person right now. We'd ask you all about the battles you've faced. We'd get to hear about the pain you've encountered, if you'd share it with us.

We would say that we know your challenges haven't been easy, but we believe God has hope on the other side. We'd tell you that

God is with you and will never leave you. You won't have to do this alone.

We also want you to know that it's not going to feel discouraging forever. All your big dreams, all your heart's desires for a relationship—maybe God gave them to you for a reason.

The mask you've put on may have helped you get where you are right now, but perhaps it's no longer serving you. It's time to let your heart encounter the Prince in a whole new way. A beautiful love story could be right in front of you, one that's even better than you dreamed.

The mask you've put on may no longer be serving you. It's time to let your heart encounter the Prince.

Will you come on this journey with us to find out if wholehearted love is possible and worth what it takes to get there?

When we find healing from past pain or trauma, we can experience wholehearted love as God intended. We can grow to love God, others, and ourselves more completely. We can have our hearts be fully known, fully seen, and fully loved.

WHAT ARE YOU LOOKING FOR?

We're so glad you're here. You're courageous to be diving into the subject of loving others, yourself, and God more wholeheartedly. If you are still unsure about whether this is the right book for you, consider whether any of the following scenarios describe you:

> You have a great desire to be married, but your love life hasn't yet worked out the way you hoped it would.
>
> You are single and don't know if you want to be married, but you want to love with your whole heart.
>
> You are dating, and you want to know how to tell who is a safe person to give your heart to and who isn't.

You are almost engaged, engaged, or newly married and want
to keep your relationship healthy and thriving over time.
You don't desire to get married, or get married again, but you
want to have a loving, open heart toward your friends,
family, and community.
You are happily married but desire even more connection
with your spouse.
Your marriage seems very difficult, and you want to feel more
seen and loved by your spouse.
You are divorced, your heart is shattered, and you want
reassurance that there is still hope for a better relationship
in the future.

If you fit into any of those circumstances, you're in the right
place! Your heart is so very precious to Jesus. He cares about you
more than you could know. He wants to heal all the hurting, disappointed, or walled off places so you can be more fully seen and
loved and be loved in a safe way.

The emotions that accompany the situations suggested above
are complex. Any or all of these thoughts may be going through
your mind:

I feel alone and I long for a relationship.
I'm just out of a bad relationship and I'm still not over it.
My expectations are not being met.
My relationship is not going the way I want it to.
I keep thinking about my ex.
I keep going back to someone who's wrong for me or ending
up with people who are noncommittal.
I must be crazy—I don't understand why I keep doing what
I'm doing even though I'm unhappy.
I wish I could be authentically myself in a relationship and
feel happy with who I am.

I feel like I'll never find the one for me.

If you are married, you may wrestle with these questions:

Does he still love me? Am I still desirable to him? Is this just
the way it will be forever now?

How do I win back her heart?

I've experienced broken trust in my marriage. How can I
regain trust in my spouse?

The details of your situation and the emotions you are experiencing may vary from these possibilities, but it all comes down to a few basic questions:

Why do I keep making bad decisions?

Is there something wrong with me?

Am I worthy of love?

Will I ever feel safe?

Will anyone ever see and love the real me?

Will I lose my identity in a relationship?

Will I just get hurt?

What's the point?

PAST BAGGAGE

When I (Stefanie) first met one of my clients, Zara, her protective mask was as firmly in place as if it were forged to her. I fully understood from the stories she told of her past that this was her way of coping with the pain. I had an immense amount of compassion for her.

Zara's dating profile was filled with pictures of her that didn't leave much to the imagination. She wondered why she kept attracting immature men who weren't really interested in a serious relationship. She had seen beautiful women dressed in a certain way get the "hottest guys," and she thought that was what would make her happy. But time after time, she was left feeling used.

She acted like sleeping around didn't faze her, but as she shared more of her story, her distress flowed from her eyes like a waterfall.

"Why doesn't anyone commit to me?" she wondered aloud. "I always thought if I gave them sex, they would keep me around. But now I'm finding that it's not the case."

My heart ached for her. This woman, who I could tell had the biggest heart and beautiful dreams, wanted a man who was loyal and kind. Someone she could trust enough to have a family with. Someone who would be there for her.

Zara initially told me she had never been in a serious relationship. But then she described a four-year "friendship" with a guy she met at college. She referred to him as her best friend. And she gave him everything. She did his laundry and took care of things he needed help with. She was always there for him, and she even paid for different things. They sometimes spent the night together, but he also had several girlfriends during those four years.

But then—just days after the two of them spent a romantic weekend away together—he told her that he was going to be a dad with another woman. It wasn't until that moment that she was finally ready to be done with him.

And maybe done with love for good.

She told herself, *I'm so strong, it doesn't bother me. I don't need anyone. Men are all terrible. Who needs a relationship after all?*

But I could see through her bravado. I understood all too well why she was feeling this way. She believed that closing herself off would enable her to push beyond the torture her shattered and bruised heart had been through.

Her dreams were withering, but I saw a glimpse of hope.

"What if something could be different?" I asked softly. "What if you can heal from this and be set up for an amazing relationship in the future?"

BEAUTY FROM ASHES

Dear friend, it might feel easier to give up hoping for something beautiful. But God is in the business of making beauty appear from ashes. He hasn't forgotten about your heart's desire. He has made you a masterpiece. The future He has for you is filled with hope and good things. But will you allow yourself to dream a little? Will you allow yourself to anticipate brighter days on the other side of pain? Hope can be daunting, but it can change everything.

Your life can be different and we're going to show you how. First, in the remainder of this chapter, we'll help you define the type of life you want for yourself. You'll think through the kinds of relationships you're looking for, both with others and with God. Sometimes, though, toxic thoughts can keep you from achieving the life you desire. We'll help you uncover some of those in the next chapter. A little later, we'll look at the coping mechanisms that are often used to cover pain, and we'll consider how they might be at work in your own relationships. We'll also talk about how toxic thoughts lead to behaviors and cycles that prevent you from living wholeheartedly.

Too often, when we are in pain, we forget how much God loves us, so we will spend some time unpacking the idea of God's goodness, and how He displays His love in the good and the bad. Sometimes, even when we know God cares so much for us, and even when we have come to understand the toxic thoughts that have held us back, we may come up against a problem that

It might feel easier to give up hoping for something beautiful. But God is in the business of making beauty from ashes.

overwhelms us. We will talk about what happens when you are at the end of your rope, and how you have a choice to do something different.

In later chapters, we will give you the truth, not only about who God says you are but about the future He has in store for you. We will show you how to believe the truth and take action surrounded by the truth. You'll also discover the secret weapon for combating the toxic thoughts you will come across. Lastly, we will show you how to move forward, feeling known, seen, and loved. All of this will help you to find healing from past pain or trauma so you can experience wholehearted love as God intended.

Throughout this book, we will illustrate these points to you by sharing vulnerably the emotional suffering that we have experienced and observed in different romantic relationships in our own lives as well as those of our clients. We will also cover topics such as the pain of family relationships, broken dreams, cheating, sexual abuse, and pregnancy loss. Most important, we'll anticipate the triumphs, healing, and amazing things God can do despite any pain that you may have gone through.

Fast-forward a year later after working with Zara. She incorporated the concepts we share in this book into her life, and Stefanie worked with her one-on-one and then in group coaching (via Zoom). God started revealing all the reasons she had done the things that she did. He healed her shame. He relieved her pain. She is now engaged to the most amazing man, someone who treats her with love and respect. She changed her approach to relationships and got much better results this time.

What started her on the right foot was hope. Hope that her heart could heal. Hope that the men who used her weren't the only ones out there. Remember, there are over eight billion people in the world. There are bound to be some good men among them.

She knew *why* she was showing up to our group every week.

She had a vision of a life that she didn't yet see but still hoped for. As the author of the book of Hebrews says, "Faith is confidence in what we hope for and assurance about what we do not see" (11:1).

Zara believed those words, and she started to let herself be loved deeply by the God of the universe.

ENVISIONING YOUR DREAM

"Welcome to Hollywood! What's your dream?"

This is one of the iconic lines from the movie *Pretty Woman*. A man walking through the streets yells it out among the people walking along, and the line rings like a familiar song to those who watch the film.

We used to live in Los Angeles, and you can feel the dreams in the air there. There's such a sense of hope, aspiration, and purpose. We've never been anywhere like it. As you walk around, you can see those who have achieved it all—money, fame—living in the mansions that line the streets of the Hollywood Hills. But you can also see people who once had dreams but are now homeless, hurt, and crushed by the weight of this world.

The line "What's your dream?" resonates with many who see the film, causing them to reflect and remember what they set out for and what their dreams are made of.

In the same way, we have to ask you: What's *your* dream? What have you always longed for? Is it to have a partner to share life with? Or perhaps a fairy-tale romance fit for a top-ten spot on Netflix? It might even be finding your true purpose—why God created you—but you haven't been able to sort through the mess in your life to find just what that is.

No matter what your dream is, we have found that identifying exactly what you want and setting a plan and goals allows you to take action and actually achieve it.

It's like a battle plan for war. Arranging the armies in the right places gives one side a tactical advantage and a way to win the fight. Those who do the best planning can beat even the strongest army.

So what is your dream? We want to help you figure out what you are looking for and why it's important. Essentially, it's your "why" for pursuing wholehearted love.

Loving others can be so messy. Pain from bad experiences in the past, insecurities about how we were made, the kinds of people (or lack thereof) in our lives, uncertainty about whether we are "qualified" for a loving relationship—all of these may put up barriers in your heart. They feel like good reasons for hesitating to get too deeply involved, which will ultimately keep you from wholehearted love.

At some time in your life, you've had a dream or desire for what a fulfilling relationship would look like, but perhaps unmet expectations have become a huge area of pain for you. Maybe you've lowered your standards significantly because you're not finding the type of person you always envisioned. Without firm goals and boundaries in place, you may be tempted to accept people who cheat on you or treat you poorly in other ways.

Or maybe you've been closing yourself off to your spouse. You feel as if part of you is dying. It seems easier to put up walls than to be vulnerable to further hurt.

And maybe you feel this spreading into your relationship with God. If you're honest, perhaps your relationship with Him feels only surface level. You've hidden parts of yourself from Him, and you aren't encountering His love like you have in the past. You want to feel His love again.

Often, there is a huge difference between what we think we want and what will truly bring us joy, fulfillment, and peace. Every successful business has a mission statement and business plan. The purpose of these is to ensure that all personnel will continue conducting business in accordance with the company's purpose and vision, whether in times of success or setback. Having this mission statement keeps them on brand, focused, motivated, and able to communicate the mission to others.

We have found that many people haven't had the mission and tools they need for their relationships to succeed long-term. It is so important to plan in a positive way, to plan for success, to plan for purpose, and, in essence, to put a stake in the ground and say, "This is what I want, and I am going to do what I need to in order to get there!"

You're here, reading this book, for a reason. If you truly want to change the course of your current or future relationships, the best place to start is by creating your personal plan or "mission statement." We like to call it a "My Why" statement. It is a statement of what you want out of life and why you are willing to do what it takes to achieve it. To put it plainly, it answers the question, Why do you want to live wholeheartedly?

In order to come up with a "My Why" statement, we believe it's important to carefully think through the following four questions. They will help you to accurately and thoroughly state your "Why."

1. Do you know how God sees you?

Our relationships affect every single aspect of our lives. And our hearts come with us everywhere, whether we like it or not, whether we try to shut them down or not. We can't remove who we are and how we love from anything else we do. But if we truly understand how God sees us, there's no reason for us to close off our hearts from our relationships and our lives.

Can you imagine for a second how God sees you? He sees you as someone He cares enough about that He sent His one and only Son to die for you. He sees only the very best, purest version of you, with all your sins wiped away as far as the east is from the west (see Psalm 103:12).

God wants us to walk with Him so we can be the fullest version of the person He created us to be. When you understand this, you can carry yourself with humility as His beloved. When you know you're loved beyond imagination by the one who created heaven and earth, you can walk authentically from a deep place in your soul that can't be shaken. How would that feel?

2. Why is it important to you to love with your whole heart?

Wholehearted love is exactly that, loving with every part of your heart—nothing hidden, allowing yourself and someone else to have access to all of you. No walls, no masks, no filters. Just the raw and real you.

Think about what it would feel like to be loved fully and unconditionally for who you are at your core. Why is that important to you?

If you could fast-forward to your absolute dream relationship, can you describe what it would look like? How would your future boyfriend/girlfriend/spouse treat you? What would you do together? How would being in that relationship affect the rest of your life?

These are all great questions and important to think about. Knowing what you want allows you to make important decisions. It helps you to see ways that you can set up your relationship to be more like your dream. It enables you to know what you would allow or be willing to put up with, or what you would put a stop to.

3. What kind of values will you hold on to in your dream relationship?

Like us, you have very likely compromised about something in your life. Perhaps you, too, have allowed certain values into relationships that you now regret. Thinking about this question gives you the opportunity to identify and set boundaries based on the values you are going to stick to and give priority in your current or future relationship.

Values can play a huge part in our compatibility with another person, so understanding what is attractive to us, what would need to be worked on, or what would be a deal-breaker is key in understanding your relationships and loving wholeheartedly.

4. How would loving and living wholeheartedly impact the rest of your life?

Imagine just for a short moment what it would be like to get to heaven and meet Jesus. You feel His glory and goodness. All the baggage is gone. And you realize that so much of the burden you carried didn't have to be with you on earth. You could have experienced a little taste of heaven more often.

Picture that heavenly version of yourself, free from all the chains, standing in the most beautiful light. Think of what that version of yourself, free from insecurity, has to bless the world with—your love and tenderness.

Think of how that bright version of yourself would be able to have relationships with others. How would it feel to connect on an even deeper level of beautiful intimacy with the right person? And then, how would it impact the rest of your life to love in this way?

No matter what stage of life you are in, you find yourself in this book for such a time as this. So today we encourage you to think about why you want to love wholeheartedly. What is calling you to this deeper sense of love and fulfillment? Allow God to shape you as you walk through this journey with us.

MAKING IT PERSONAL

At the end of each chapter, we will include a section designed to help take you a little deeper into the ideas we have explored together. To receive the most benefit from this experience, we encourage you to read through the Scripture verses and answer the questions, prayerfully considering areas where God may be prompting you toward growth and change. We are so glad you are here, and we pray you will gain life-changing insights as you continue.

Scripture to Apply

Read the following verses and note what they say about how God views you and the kind of life He wants you to have. Summarize what you see in these verses in the space provided below.

> LORD, the God of Israel, there is no God like you in heaven or on earth—you who keep your covenant of love with your servants who continue wholeheartedly in your way. (2 Chronicles 6:14)

> Serve wholeheartedly, as if you were serving the Lord, not people. (Ephesians 6:7)

> God created man in his own image, in the image of God he created him; male and female he created them. (Genesis 1:27, ESV)

> We are his workmanship, created in Christ Jesus for good works, which God prepared beforehand, that we should walk in them. (Ephesians 2:10, ESV)

I have told you these things, so that in me you may have peace. In this world you will have trouble. But take heart! I have overcome the world. (John 16:33)

Because my servant Caleb has a different spirit and follows me wholeheartedly, I will bring him into the land he went to, and his descendants will inherit it. (Numbers 14:24)

Questions to Consider

1. Has your past or current relationship had negative patterns that you don't want to continue? Describe them below.

2. How would it feel to love with your entire heart and to be completely safe and comfortable?

3. If you could be fully yourself and know how cherished and accepted you are, why would this change other aspects of your life?

4. How will loving the right people with your whole heart have a positive impact on the following:

- Your happiness

  _____

- Your future or current spouse

  _____

- Your future or current children

  _____

- Your community

  _____

- Your legacy

  _____

- The decisions you make for your future

  _____

Call to Action

Create a short "My Why" statement for yourself. Review the four questions on pages 15 to 17 and think about why you want to go on this journey of becoming wholehearted. What areas of your life will get better because you do? What will keep you motivated so you don't pause this journey?

Here is a sample statement that might help you with creating your own:

> "I do this because I want to be wholly myself, the way God intended me to be. I want to be healed from past pain and walk in freedom so I can more fully give and receive love. I don't want to be stuck when I could be free. This will have a positive effect on my joy, my health, my knowledge of God's goodness, and my ability to reflect God's light and love to others."

My Why statement:

Now, read your "My Why" statement every morning and/or night. Remind yourself of what is important to you. Use it as motivation to keep you on this journey that could change the trajectory of your life.

2

When Thoughts Turn Toxic

OVERCOMING THE FALSE BELIEFS
THAT STAND IN YOUR WAY

CALEB'S STORY: THREE TUMBLING DOMINOES

I sat in an old brown chair, powerless to get up, incapable of feeling, and unable to grasp that the future I had dreamed of was blowing up all around me. I couldn't believe what had just happened.

Within days, I had lost three of the things that had shaped my identity—EVERYTHING I thought was important to me, and everything I had worked my entire life to get. It felt like a wildfire had swept in, destroying all in its path and leaving the charred and flattened landscape behind as a reminder of hopes and dreams dashed by despair.

The smell of the old leather chair was like a mist that I couldn't escape. It was a quiet reminder of failure and the end of my dream. Distraction became my friend, and I retreated into the darkness of my mind.

To understand the intensity of my pain, we have to go back to the start.

I have always loved basketball. My earliest memories are filled with balls of all kinds. I would play for hours, even under the scorching sun or pouring rain. I felt alive. In the summer, I'd be outside from dawn till dusk, dreaming of making the last-second shot like Michael Jordan to win the championship.

I dreamed of playing professionally, showcasing the abilities and passion that God had instilled in me from a young age. Nothing sounded more fulfilling. I dedicated my life to developing my craft and getting to that dream.

When something frustrating happened at home or school, I would grab my basketball, sometimes in the middle of the night, and shoot until my sobs were drowned out by the sound of the swishing net, even if it took hundreds of shots.

Being *good* wasn't in my list of possible realities. I had to be the best or nothing at all, so I worked hard at whatever I did.

I had a successful high school career, and in junior college I earned all-conference honors my first year. Eventually I earned a scholarship to play for my dream school. It was a small Christian college in Southern California that has always been known for its basketball program. I was thrilled to move my dream toward reality.

God, it seems, had different plans.

My first year on campus was challenging. I didn't play as much as I wanted to, and my experience on the team wasn't what I expected. But I continued to work hard, and I knew that my chance would come.

The First Domino Falls

Senior year came and there was hope in the air. I truly felt like I was making a difference on the team. The coaches were starting to take notice and had pulled me aside a couple of times to say that they saw the work I was putting in. They said if I kept it up, opportunities would abound.

We had our first two scrimmages of the season with two local Division 1 teams. In each game I had over twenty points and played well, even coming off the bench. Eventually, I knew, the starting job was mine.

But then it all changed. One day in practice, I turned the corner during a drill, and my back gave out. I collapsed on the floor, puzzled at why I hadn't been able to make this routine move to the basket for a slam dunk. As I lay on the floor in pain, staring at the black ceiling of the gym, my hopes and dreams flashed before my eyes. I knew it was over, but I didn't want to believe it.

The trainers took me into their office, and they said it was most likely a bulging disc and a pinched nerve in my back. It was unbelievably painful to walk, much less get around on the court. They said that the season—the last one of my college career—was likely over for me.

I vividly remember going home that day feeling numb. The house I lived in, which normally was full of life (I had seven roommates) became a place of quiet and sorrow as I seemed to hear only my own thoughts aloud. I pictured every sacrifice, every moment of life I had given up to pursue this dream. The parties, the experiences, the school clubs, the study abroad opportunities—I had missed out on all of them in the name of pursuing this dream of mine and trying to honor God.

Each minute felt like a year as I sat in misery, completely shaken by what had just happened. What was I left with? Picking up the pieces of a shattered dream. Each piece cut through me as I tried to put them back together. I had never felt such pain in my entire life. It was like a bad dream that just went on and on, and I couldn't wake up.

The Second Domino

My birthday came soon after my injury, and I was looking forward to that because my family did a great job celebrating milestones for each of us. My parents always went over the top with presents and with honoring my brothers and me. I hoped it would take my mind off my pain.

In addition, my girlfriend was going to throw my birthday party this year. We had been together for six years, and I thought we'd be together the rest of our lives. We had dated since high school and had even chosen the same college. The party was going to be at her grandparents' home on the Sunday after my birthday. They had a huge house fairly close to the university, so people would easily be able to come and have a good time.

My birthday, on Thursday, was going well. My family and my girlfriend and I went out to dinner at my favorite place to eat in Southern California, In-N-Out, and then we went back to my parents' house.

As I sat on the old wooden chair in their living room, feeling optimistic for the first time in a few days, I was given this amazing *Archaeological Study Bible* for my birthday. I loved it. It felt light, yet it had references to all parts of the Bible and their historical significance. Then, with a few words from my parents, that book turned into a two-ton weight in my hands.

"Caleb," they said, "we are so sorry to tell you this, but today your grandfather was walking out of the hospital after a good checkup, and he had a heart attack in the parking lot and died."

Speechless, I was crushed, again. I felt like a boxer who had been knocked to the ground and was slowly getting up, only to take another massive punch to the face. I had never lost someone that significant to me, so this news hit me hard.

The Final Domino

At this point I was reeling. Dazed and confused, I thought to myself, *What else could possibly go wrong?* I just wanted to get to the weekend to celebrate and hopefully get some encouragement and hope.

The party was okay. Most of the people there were my girlfriend's college friends and some of my friends from the dorm. I thought, *There is some light at the end of the tunnel.*

Little did I know that the last domino was about to fall. The day after the party, my girlfriend asked to have a chat with me. She was my first love, the girl I had grown up with, and the one I had gone to school dances with. I thought, *This could be promising. Maybe she is ready to take the next step.*

But after we drove somewhere to talk, she gave me the news that she no longer wanted to be with me.

Okay, this was a hit below the belt. It just felt cruel, like everyone was in on some plan to make me miserable and take away *all* my dreams. I felt like a gazelle being attacked by a pride of lions, all coming at me at once. I had been hanging on, but this largest lion finally took me out. I couldn't believe what I was hearing.

When she dropped me off at home, I was a mess, crying uncontrollably as she drove away. I sat on the street corner across from our house and wept for hours. Everything had been stripped from me, it seemed. I felt like I had nothing left. The shattered pieces of my heart, already all over the ground, now felt as if they were being crushed under a cement roller. My trust was broken, both in my girlfriend and in God. I had trusted them both up until that point. Now it seemed that it had all been a waste.

Having these three dominoes fall so quickly triggered me to accept some deeply detrimental thoughts about myself, others, and God. I believed that I was clearly *not good enough.* Instead of trusting that God had a plan for me, I started accepting untrue core thoughts about myself and my purpose. I believed *God is holding out on me.* I believed *I'm a failure.* And I believed *No one will care about me.*

THE TRUTH ABOUT TOXIC THOUGHTS

Now that you have decided on your "My Why" statement in chapter 1, you have a great idea of why you are reading this book and what you are looking for in a relationship. You are on your way toward finding healing from past pain or trauma, so you can experience wholehearted love as God intended. Before we jump into how to make that happen, there's something you need to be aware of. It's the invisible reason that relationships might not be working out for you.

Many times, there are things underneath the surface that keep us from having a thriving relationship. These can be the effects of a past breakup, childhood abuse, bullying, or any number of other distressing experiences. These old pains can repeatedly come up in our minds and cause us to think things that aren't true about ourselves, others, and God. We refer to this as having "toxic thoughts."

A *toxic thought* is a lie against your core identity, against God's identity, and/or against the identity of others.[1] It stems from a violation of love and trust and/or from pain we have suffered. We put our faith in a person, and something they do or say (or fail to do or say) blindsides us and causes emotional injury. The experience leads us to believe something untrue, and when we accept the untruth, it enforces a toxic thought.

Pain we experience can come from anyone or any circumstance. Anyone that we allow to speak into our lives can trigger us to believe toxic thoughts. When we respond by jumping to conclusions about who we are, who God is, and who others are, based on what we see or hear, we are creating belief systems that may or may not be accurate. The death of someone we care about, a divorce in our family, trauma, sickness—all of these can trigger us to believe a toxic thought to the core of our identity.

The pain can hit the worst when we see it as being caused by those we should be able to trust the most or whom we put the most trust in—the ones we should be able to feel safe with. Often, those we perceive as having let us down have titles such as God, parent, grandparent, teacher, best friend, coach, boyfriend, or spouse. These are the ones who are supposed to be *for* us, to be on our side. They are not supposed to harm us but help us. In our hurting world, though, hurt people hurt people, no matter what title they hold. Our toxic thoughts stem from a violation of love or trust—including the times we feel like we have failed ourselves.

Toxic thoughts can end up feeling much more like truth than the actual truth. Because we live in a fallen world, our perception of reality is faulty. We can be quick to believe our experiences and what others say (or what we think they are implying), especially if we don't know to believe something different.

How do we know if we have toxic thoughts? And how were they formed in the first place?

Each human who has walked on this earth has most likely experienced one or many toxic thoughts. They are not merely emotions. They are instead the beliefs that can *trigger* many of the negative emotions we feel. Our primary emotions are happiness, sadness, disgust, fear, surprise, and anger. When we feel sadness, fear, anxiety, loneliness, confusion, emptiness, longing, etc., we will often find toxic thoughts underneath them.

Here's how Dr. Terry Hargrave describes some of the toxic ideas we can have about ourselves and how they impact our lives:

While the primary emotions of feeling unloved or unsafe are not able to be verbalized in infancy or early childhood, they are nonetheless apparent as the child is unattached, fails to thrive, or is in constant distress. . . . In adulthood, individuals express the primary emotion related to feeling unloved using various terms: unloved, unworthy, insignificant, alone, worthless, devalued, defective, inadequate, rejected, unacceptable, hopeless, unwanted, . . . and others.[2]

Consider this example of how toxic thoughts come about: each time you get an email from your boss, your heart drops. Although you've been a teacher at the same school for the last five years, and in all that time you've only received one negative email, that one email still haunts you. It was that moment, three years ago, when a parent-teacher conference went horribly wrong. The parent lashed out at you, and you responded with unkindness. The principal (your boss) sent you a strongly worded email the next day, and you had a rough meeting with her. Since that incident, you've received nothing but kind emails or normal updates from your boss, just like it had been before that conflict.

But your heart rate still increases every time you see your boss's name in your inbox. You start to overcompensate and stay later at work, and you say yes to all the extra things she asks you to do.

The reason you are feeling anxious in this scenario is that the initial email led to a toxic thought about your identity that now gets triggered every time you see the boss's name.

The toxic thought it triggers is *I'm not good enough* or *I'm a failure.* Your brain rushes to the thought, *Oh no, they're going to tell me I did something wrong again.*

In order to start changing this pathway, you have to identify what you are feeling. You have to acknowledge, *Wow, when I get an email from my boss, it triggers the toxic thought, "I'm not good enough."*

That's a very strong belief to hold. Of course you would feel anxious when you are believing such a negative statement about yourself. Giving yourself grace in the moment, acknowledging the primary emotion and the toxic thought that was triggered, is the first step to breaking free from these toxic thoughts.

We don't want to get too far ahead here, but the next time you feel anxious or sad, try tracing back what caused you to have the reaction you did, and what toxic thought you might be believing underneath it. It will be so helpful to understand this about yourself as you continue reading.

Often, it's those toxic thoughts that we believe that cause us to close off a part of our heart.

UNCOVERING OUR TRUE IDENTITY

One of our favorite shows is called *Once Upon a Time*. Have you seen it? It's about Disney fairy-tale characters who have fallen under a curse and are stuck in our world, but with new identities and fake memories. The curse also keeps them from remembering the love of their life or their parents or children. They are separated from the things they love most and don't even know it. They are living in a real world, but they aren't their true selves.

The "savior" in this story is Emma. She is the product of "true love"—Snow White and Prince Charming are her parents—but she has no idea.

Prince Charming and Snow White loved their daughter with all their heart. But when she was born, they had to put her through a wardrobe into our world to save her from the curse. They knew that she was the savior and that her best chance of surviving was to go through the wardrobe alone. Emma grew up going from one foster home to the next, with no idea who her real parents were.

On her twenty-eighth birthday, the son Emma had given up for adoption comes to find her. His name is Henry, and he is one of the few "believers" who know the truth about the curse. He tries desperately to get Emma to see her true identity, but the fairy-tale world seems far-fetched. It's much easier to believe that her parents abandoned her than to believe they were trying to save her and others out of their great love and sacrifice.

Isn't that just like us? We read the Bible and hear about Jesus coming to save the world, we hear about heaven and our true identity—what God has called us to—but it's oh so much easier to believe we are unwanted orphans.

In the show, it's only when the "savior" breaks the curse that the characters are able to see clearly. They remember who they really are. They know who they really love.

The curse of sin has done something so similar to us. In Emma's experience of life, she constructed ways to view herself, others, and the world. Growing up in the foster homes, she felt used, abandoned, and alone. People used her to get that government check, and when caring for her got to be too much of a hassle, they gave her up and she was put into another home. She looked for love in the arms of men, and she was let down when she learned that they could break their word and her trust.

She learned through experience that she had to get by on her own and look out only for herself. Loving people is dangerous. She learned that people use others and that she couldn't trust anyone. Deeper still, she believed the toxic thought that she was unwanted, unworthy, always alone, and unlovable. She could base this in truth since she was constantly and consistently abandoned and unwanted. Everything Emma experienced pointed to this being the truth about her identity, other people's identity, and the lack of a "higher power."

Although almost all the evidence pointed to these toxic thoughts being true, they weren't. In reality, she was so cherished and loved. She was the daughter of a king and queen who wanted her and gave up so much for her. Her dad fought almost to his death to keep her safe.

Our stories and yours are very similar to Emma's. Our world beats us down. We are surrounded by people and circumstances that constantly break our love and trust. The toxic thoughts we believe about ourselves, others, and God might have started with a seed of doubt, but they can quickly grow into the biggest tree, with roots that overrun our thoughts, beliefs, and lives because our experience points to the toxic thoughts as truth.

But Jesus came to save us. He is the Savior of our world, and unlike Emma, He knew His identity. He heard His Father's voice, and He knew the mission He was called to on this earth. Jesus knew that each of us would be born cursed to sin. That we would feel the pain and shame and lack of knowing our true identity. That we would search our whole lives trying to find who we really are. That we would look for love and meaning in unsatisfying and harmful places.

Jesus came to save us. He knew we would search our whole lives to find who we really are.

When we choose to believe toxic thoughts about ourselves, it keeps us from discovering the identity that we are destined to have. Like Emma, we continually substitute lies for the truth of God, and we let those toxic thoughts run rampant.

The two of us have believed toxic thoughts about ourselves. Deep-seated toxic thoughts have become implanted inside of us when we have experienced pain. And they led us down paths neither of us expected to go.

The good news is that the toxic thoughts we believe are, in fact, lies. They aren't true, and they don't need to remain as part of our identity.

PAVING NEW PATHWAYS

One of our favorite things to do together is hiking. On a recent trip to Los Angeles, our former home, we tried to go hiking every day. Hiking in LA is beautiful, and we especially love to hike at Griffith Park. There is just something magical about the sandy trails, curving effortlessly against the slope of the mountains, leading you, calling you to the peak, where the view takes your breath away. You'll find close to 360-degree views across the beautiful downtown area, the iconic observatory, the deep blue Pacific Ocean, and the snowcapped peaks of Mount Baldy. It is quite astounding.

Think about those paths we follow on a hike. At some time in the past, someone broke the trail for them, and as more and more people walked along them, they became permanent. They give us a clear direction to follow, and they lead us to the location that we set out for. We don't go on a hike in Griffith Park expecting that it will lead us to Central Park in New York.

In the same way, thought patterns can form pathways in our brain over time. Our brain learns to have a certain reaction when something happens to us. For instance, when someone calls us a bad name at school, we begin to think badly about ourselves. After we have been called that name over and over, we start to believe it. Our brain begins to tell us that it is true, and it happens naturally when that part of our brain is triggered. When we get older and someone says something mean about us, our brain tells us that it's probably true because of what people have told us in the past.

Most of the time we are unaware of it even happening. Our brain is on autopilot, and this is why toxic thoughts can be difficult to overcome.

So what can we do about this? To break free of those thoughts, you have to be willing to turn off autopilot and take control of the wheel.

Imagine you are standing at a trailhead. Signs point toward two different trails that you can take. One of them looks paved and cleared of brush, and it seems nice and flat to walk on. The other one looks like it has jagged branches overlapping both edges. It is unpaved and rocky, and the incline looks like the steps to Mordor— straight up. Which would you choose?

Most of us would choose the paved path, right? We'd be on that one faster than you could say, "the paved path."

But what if we told you the destination at the end of the nicely paved trail was a garbage dump? The odor would make you feel sick, and the surrounding land is filled with toxic waste that would hurt your long-term health.

And what if we told you that at the end of the unpaved path were the most beautiful ocean views you've ever seen? From the overlook you'd see aqua water (the kind they post on Instagram travel pages), with whales swimming under the surface. Nearby, a stream flows peacefully to a waterfall over the cliff into the ocean. There is a place to rest by the stream, a bed of grass like the softest pillow to lie on. The water in the stream is full of nutrients that would refresh your body, taking away any exhaustion from the journey. It even contains healing properties that could allow you to live a longer, healthier life. It would be relaxing, calm, and peaceful, and your soul would feel refreshed.

Which path would you choose now?

Would it be worth it to make that second path clearer and easier to get through, so that anytime you wanted, you could go to your beautiful, peaceful oasis?

It's the same with the pathways in our brain. Many of us have been so used to our toxic thoughts that they feel comfortable—like the paved path. But once we get to the destination, it hurts. It steals our joy and increases our stress, and in the end, that stress can lead to a shorter life span. It's killing us and our most important relationships. But it's what we've become used to.

Most of this is happening unconsciously. Triggers pop up many times a day, and we unknowingly let our brain go to the awful destination we've become so familiar with.

We have to start thinking about what we're thinking about. This is how it is possible to start paving new paths in our brain. Once developed and practiced, the new pathways become easier to believe, and the peaceful destination becomes easier to get to. Paving new pathways of freedom for our thoughts takes intentional work, but it gets much simpler over time and sets us up for long-term freedom.

Paving new pathways for our thoughts gets easier and sets us up for long-term freedom.

Are you game to travel this unpaved trail? As we stomp through the brush, the path will become more apparent. Tooling yourself with the right mindset and best practices works like a Weedwacker to clear the trail. The path will grow more beautiful, and the destination will be better than you can imagine.

To start, you have to be able to identify the toxic thoughts that you are believing. Following are some of the common ones that we ourselves have believed and that we hear from other people all the time.

Toxic thoughts about yourself:

I'm not good enough	I'm a failure
I'm unloved	I have no purpose in life
I'm unworthy	I'm ugly
I'm worthless	I'm not gifted
I'm alone	I'm unlovable

I'm an object	Others are better than me
I'm an embarrassment	My voice doesn't matter

Toxic thoughts about others:

They are worthless	They have no purpose
They don't matter	I'm better than them
They are an object	

Toxic thoughts about God:

God doesn't love me	God is holding out on me
God is not good	

Are any of these standing out to you?

The two of us have worked to overcome many of these thoughts and to pave new paths in our brains, and we want to help you do the same. We will share more about how you can do this as you keep reading.

STEFANIE'S STORY: "YOU'RE AN EMBARRASSMENT"

He was my favorite teacher. I had hoped and wished to get Mr. Saperstein for the fourth grade, and he was even better than all the kids said! He was funny and kind, and I learned a lot from him. And he gave us a whole hour each day for quiet reading time.

During this time, we got to sit at our desks or in a corner of the room and read any book we wanted. The "good kids" sat at their desks. The "cool kids" sat in the corners and talked with their friends quietly. I wanted to be a good student. I didn't want to get in trouble like the kids in the corner often did, so I sat at my desk, reading silently.

One of our silent reading times was interrupted by a door opening in the front of the room. Ms. Darlene came in and walked past all of us to Mr. Saperstein's desk, which was right behind mine. I heard Ms. Darlene and Mr. Saperstein whispering about one of the students in our class. I turned my head to look, too curious for my own good.

"Stefanie, want to pull up a chair so you can join our conversation?" Mr. Saperstein said loudly in a sarcastic voice. Everyone in the class stared at me. I wished more than anything that I could turn invisible right at that moment.

"No, I'm sorry," I said sheepishly, holding back tears with all my might.

My sensitive little heart had never taken sarcasm well. The message I got from this exchange was *You're an embarrassment.* Although this was one of the first times I felt this strong toxic thought come up, it wasn't the last.

I did so much throughout my days at school to hide the undeniable fact in my head that I was an embarrassment. No matter how hard I tried, the feeling would pop back up with every trigger. Being dyslexic, I prayed I would not get called on for "popcorn" reading aloud or for writing on the chalkboard. I feared my being *an embarrassment* and *not good enough* would be seen by all.

I'm sure Mr. Saperstein had no idea of the effect his sarcastic words had on that fourth grader. Looking back, I'm sure he didn't think I was an embarrassment. But whether or not the trusted person meant to hurt us, their subliminal or overt messages set a chord that can be struck again without notice.

I tried hard to hide the parts of myself that were *an embarrassment* and *not good enough.*

I remember sitting in the corner during the next reading time. No need to be so good. And no need to read. I figured out that I'm actually more hidden when I follow along with the crowd. Why try so hard? If I just act cool and pretend I don't care, I won't feel like such an embarrassment next time.

WHY YOU CLOSED YOUR HEART

Perhaps you can remember similar stories from your childhood. Can you think of a toxic thought you believed that caused you to change or hide part of yourself?

If you are like us, you have experienced many moments of pain that have led you to where you are now. Maybe you started with a dream of true love, or the dream of being special and unique, loved by your teachers, parents, and friends for just who you are. But somewhere on the road, you've lost part of yourself.

Maybe it was an F on a test. Maybe it was something one of your classmates said or did to you at school. Maybe it was the betrayal of a friend or words from a parent.

Maybe your boyfriend cheated on you, or the girl you thought you were going to marry decided that you needed a break and then dumped you. And you started to close off your heart.

I'm a failure was now your identity after that F.

I'm fat and ugly is now your identity after a classmate called you names.

I'm always going to be alone, after the betrayal of a friend.

I'm not lovable, after someone in your family leaves.

How could anyone love me? after you were cheated on.

If they don't love me anymore, maybe no one will love me, after the breakup.

All the violations of love and trust, the heartbreaks and broken dreams, were the building blocks for a closed off heart. They walled off your heart piece by piece until there was nothing left to be seen.

It was the safest thing to do. You could no longer bear the thought of putting yourself out there again. The one person you gave yourself to took advantage of you and left you behind, with no explanation. Or the dream you had fell apart because you took a wrong turn.

The toxic thoughts begin to creep in, as in the story of Emma, and they work like mortar in between the blocks, making the wall around your heart stronger and harder to break through.

Wholehearted love might seem like a dream for a fairy tale, something we see only in the movies or in posts from people who act fake on Instagram. It seems more realistic that you will have to settle for someone in order to not be alone.

One of our clients, Rodger, had always dreamed of falling in love, but he was pretty shy and had never been on a date. He wanted to find "his person" but didn't really know how.

Rodger met a girl through school who he got along with very well. They would talk and hang out, and became friends very quickly. Rodger really liked spending time with her at school and began to develop feelings for his new friend. As time went by, Rodger began to fall in love with her and wanted to find out if those feelings were mutual. Maybe they would be like the couples he dreamed about. He decided to officially ask his friend to coffee. She said yes, and they set a date.

Rodger was so excited. He planned his outfit, found new clothes, and couldn't wait for the date. When it finally came, Rodger decided to get there early to grab a seat. He sat down by a window, with his nervousness building.

Ten minutes went by with no sign of her. Twenty, nothing yet. Forty, she still wasn't there. Rodger checked his phone in case she had texted that she would be late. Nothing.

After about an hour, Rodger got up and went home. He texted his friend to see what had happened and never heard back. Ever. She had ghosted him completely.

What seemed like it would be the best day ever became one of the worst. And the toxic thoughts began to creep in. *Did you really think she'd be into you? You're so stupid for believing that you are capable of being loved! You won't ever find your person.*

The toxic thoughts of *you are unlovable, no one will ever like you, you are stupid, you are worthless* became a driving force of his new identity.

And more of Rodger's experiences started to prove this new identity as fact. Falling deeper and deeper away from his true self, Rodger almost never recovered. The truth when put up against the pain didn't add up. People told him that he was "a child of God," but his experience said that he was "worthless." He chose to close off his heart to love, and the toxic thoughts became a new normal.

Sound familiar?

Thankfully, this isn't the end of Rodger's story. As he identifies the toxic thoughts that have sidetracked his pursuit of love, it's just the beginning. In the same way, we know there's so much hope for you, too, over each and every toxic thought and all the reasons they are there in the first place. We believe God wants to restore to you what has been lost and broken.

HOPE BEYOND THE PAIN

We know this is a difficult topic and thinking about these things isn't easy. But these thoughts and experiences are there in each of us and are affecting every area of our lives, whether we're willing to look at them or not. Let's be coura-geous and willing to see what could be defining our lives without our realiz-ing it. Uncovering the toxic thoughts that hold us back is the first step to full healing and wholehearted love.

Let's be courageous and willing to see the toxic thoughts that could be defining our lives.

We get it: your pain is real. What you have experienced, we really wish you never had to go through. What you deal with on a daily basis may be heartbreaking and upsetting.

But friend, it's not the end of the story. There's hope beyond this pain. Hold on to that hope, keep reminding yourself of the "My Why" statement you wrote in chapter 1, and feel the wind that's about to bring positive change your way.

MAKING IT PERSONAL

Scripture to Apply

We invite you to read the following verses and note what they say to focus your thinking on, and what God says about your thoughts. Summarize what you see in these verses in the space provided below.

"My thoughts are not your thoughts, neither are your ways my ways," declares the LORD. (Isaiah 55:8)

O LORD, you have searched me and known me! You know when I sit down and when I rise up; you discern my thoughts from afar. You search out my path and my lying down and are acquainted with all my ways. Even before a word is on my tongue, behold, O LORD, you know it altogether. (Psalm 139:1-4, ESV)

Do not be wise in your own eyes; fear the LORD and shun evil. (Proverbs 3:7)

Finally, brothers, whatever is true, whatever is honorable, whatever is just, whatever is pure, whatever is lovely, whatever is commendable, if there is any excellence, if there is anything worthy of praise, think about these things. (Philippians 4:8, ESV)

Do not be overcome by evil, but overcome evil with good. (Romans 12:21)

Questions to Consider

1. What experiences have shaped the way you view yourself, others, and God? Why did you start to believe these things?

2. Review the lists of possible toxic thoughts on pages 36–37. What are some that you've believed about yourself, others, and God? (You may think of some that are not on these lists.)

3. What violations of love and trust do you want to see healed?

Call to Action

The next time you feel anxious, take a deep breath and follow these steps:

1. Stop and think about what you were thinking about.
2. Look over the lists of toxic thoughts earlier in this chapter.
3. Then, identify the one that you might be believing.
4. Think of an experience you have gone through that may have led you to start believing that toxic thought about yourself, others, or God.
5. Write down the experiences and toxic thoughts that come to mind right now, and be sure to write down others that occur to you as you continue reading.

From Coping to Connecting

UNDERSTANDING THE WAYS
YOU HANDLE HARDSHIP

STEFANIE'S STORY: ABSOLUTELY HOPELESS

"It's time to get up, sweetie."

Unbelievable. How can it possibly be 5:30 already? I felt as though I'd just gone to sleep a few hours ago. And now that I thought about it . . . I *had*.

I had stayed up till almost midnight talking on the phone with my best friend Nikki about the guys we liked and sharing the latest intel on which ones we thought might actually like *us*. Me? I was obsessed with Ethan. He was in tenth grade, a year above me, gorgeous, popular, the star of the football team, *and* he had stopped by my locker several times that week.

"I can't believe he likes you, Stefanie!" my friend Nikki practically squealed. "You have to go for it. He's the hottest guy in school."

Frankly, I couldn't believe it either. "It has to be some kind of practical joke," I reasoned. After all, I was the shy girl who recently got contacts instead of her big, bulky glasses. I had just begun to have a more womanly body and was growing out ever so slightly from my scrawny little frame. Although I had learned to dress more stylishly, I still felt as awkward as I did when Tommy and Evan would call me four-eyes. The image of the nerdy, scared girl on the school bus flashed through my mind.

"Come on, sweetie, let's go," Mom repeated, flipping on the light.

I sat up, stretched, and caught a glimpse of myself in the mirror—hair in tangles, pasty complexion, no figure to speak of . . . *Talk about a joke.*

Twenty minutes and a hot shower later, I plopped myself down at my white desk, in front of my little light-up vanity mirror, and started my daily makeup ritual. First the foundation, then the blush, followed by eyeshadow, mascara, a little eyeliner, and finally, lip gloss.

I glanced down at my copy of *Teen People* magazine—the confident smile and flawless complexion of Britney Spears staring back at me from the cover—then sat back and admired my handiwork.

"Not even close," I sighed. *Why can't I look like that?* I hated my hair. It was always so frizzy from the chlorine in the pool. *And why are my teeth so small?* I'd have given anything to have a big, bright, beautiful smile. I flashed my best smile and faked a flirty laugh. Yep. My best bet was to keep my mouth shut. It was just as well. I never seemed to know the right thing to say anyway.

Two days earlier, Ethan had stopped by my locker before homeroom. He told me I looked great and that he hoped I'd have a great day, and I just stood there, completely flustered, smiling closemouthed like an idiot to hide my tiny teeth, and said nothing. *Why can't I be funny and flirty like the other girls? Why am I always so shy and awkward?*

"Are you dressed yet?" Mom called down the hall.

"Yes," I lied, turning my attention to the outfit I had laid out the night before—a short skirt and a semi-crop top. It showed a little more skin than I was comfortable with, but to have any chance with this guy, I would have to pull out all the stops. What I'd do if he actually *did* ask me out I had no idea. *What if he wants to talk? What if he wants to do something other than talk?* Either way, I was in trouble. But first things first. I had to get him to like me.

"Stefanie, hurry up. The bus is going to be here any second!"

"I'm coming," I shouted back, pulling my top over my head and trying not to smudge the mascara that was already wreaking havoc with my contacts. I took one last look in the mirror.

You are hopeless. Absolutely hopeless.

As a last-ditch effort, I grabbed my Victoria's Secret "Love Spell" body mist, spritzed the air in front of me about a dozen times, closed my eyes, and walked through the wall of fragrance. *I sure hope this stuff works,* I thought as I grabbed my backpack and headed down the stairs, *because the only way a guy like that is gonna be interested in someone like me is by magic.*

That day at school, Ethan flirted with a girl who was wearing a revealing outfit and about a quarter inch of makeup and who smelled positively enchanting. But he had no idea how many "flaws" and "imperfections" all that makeup was hiding. Nor was he aware of the debilitating monologue taking place in my head. In other words . . . he had no idea who I really was.

It must be easier for guys.

CALEB'S STORY: BEER GOGGLES

What am I doing here? As I sat in the stiff wooden chair staring at a frothy pitcher of beer in one of our campus's most notorious party houses, it was all I could do to keep from gagging. I hated alcohol.

My eyes darted between the golden liquid and the golden-haired girl at the far end of the table. I wanted to impress her, but having grown up in a Christian home, I was very much out of my element. I barely even knew, let alone liked, the guys at the party. For that matter, I barely knew, let alone liked, the girl. But I was fresh on the heels of a devastating breakup, and thanks to a back injury, my basketball career had just come to an equally devastating end, so I was pretty much at rock bottom. Wallowing in the toxic thoughts *I'm not good enough* and *I'm a failure*, I didn't feel I had anything more to lose. There was nothing wrong with the girl herself, but here's the shameful truth: that night her biggest charm was that she was there and that she seemed to like me.

So here I was, getting ready to down a pitcher of beer I didn't want, to impress a girl I didn't know. But what choice did I have? I didn't want to look stupid in front of a bunch of drunken party boys I'd probably never see again.

As a chorus of "Chug, chug, chug!" broke out, I started to sweat. My eyes met the girl's, she smiled at me, and I felt . . . well . . . nothing.

Come on, Caleb, I thought, trying to psych myself up. *You've got this. For once in your life, be cool.* I grabbed the pitcher, took a deep breath, plugged my nose (which drew a few snickers from the crowd), and choked down the vile liquid, all the while pleading to God that I wouldn't throw up and make an even bigger fool of myself.

Amazingly, I didn't throw up. But that didn't stop me from making a fool of myself.

In a last-ditch attempt to cement my image as a party boy (and apparently far more committed to throwing up than I thought), I staggered out back to the trampoline, where I proceeded to do a series of backflips. This was not only dumb but given my recent back injury, flat-out dangerous. But hey . . . what girl could resist a skinny, six-foot-five-inch drunken idiot doing backflips on a trampoline? I had never done anything so stupid and careless. I could throw up now just thinking about it.

By the time the night drew to a close, I had passed out on a filthy brown sofa that reeked of stale beer and sweat. (Then again, that might have been me. It was hard to tell.) The golden-haired girl had left with someone else.

Looking back, I'm incredibly grateful that I never hooked up with a virtual stranger. If I had, I have no doubt I would have compromised everything I believed in. As Stefanie often says, "Sometimes rejection is God's protection."

THE THINGS WE HIDE

We all have our moments. Both of us have dealt with toxic thoughts that plagued us to our core. It's very likely that you can relate to some of them. As you continue to read, keep taking note of the toxic thoughts you might be believing in your own life. This can be so helpful as we move ahead on this journey toward finding healing from past pain, so we can experience wholehearted love as God intended.

So far, we've covered why you are here reading this book, the values important to you in a love relationship, and the toxic thoughts you might be believing that are getting in the way of finding "your person." As you read our stories, you can see that those toxic thoughts can get anyone stuck. Now we'll look at some of the ways we have learned to hide our toxic thoughts so we can cope with them in everyday life.

One of our favorite musicals is *The Phantom of the Opera*. If you're not familiar with it, it's about a mysterious figure who haunts a Parisian opera house and terrorizes the owners into bringing in the plays, singers, and performances he wants. Because his face is severely disfigured, he wears a mask and stays out of sight, communicating mostly via threatening letters. But one day he falls in love with a beautiful young soprano and bullies the theater owners into making her a star. At first, the young woman is mesmerized by him. But the phantom—believing she could never truly love him because of his looks—kidnaps her and tries to force her into marrying him. (It's kind of creepy when you think about it, but that's not the point.)

One of the things that has always stuck out to me (Caleb) in particular is how confident, mysterious, and dashing the phantom is. There is a sense of mystery and romance not only about his amazing voice but about the iconic white cutaway mask he wears as well. As the story unfolds, however, you realize that the mask isn't just hiding his face. It's hiding something much deeper— the pain and insecurity caused by years of bullying, rejection, and shame. Unable to accept who he really is, the phantom conceals his true identity (a brilliant musician with a beautiful voice and a tender soul) behind a mask of deception and manipulation.

Granted, this mask serves him for a while—initially, the beautiful young soprano is attracted to his musical genius. But ultimately, she rejects him. After all, how could she ever truly know or love someone who doesn't know or love himself?

Let. That. Sink. In.

Though the soundtracks for our lives weren't nearly as good, what Stefanie and I were doing in our younger days wasn't all that different from what the phantom was doing.

Many people put on masks because they need something to help with the pain.

Masks are anything we use to hide what we don't want others to see about our physical appearance, our personality, our emotions, or any other part of who we are. Masks are used to cover up our toxic thoughts. Many people put on masks because their toxic thoughts are intense and they need something to help with the pain.

We both used masks to hide our insecurities and toxic thoughts and to trick others into thinking we were something we weren't in the hope that they would like us. Caleb put on the guise of a good-time, beer-chugging party boy to hide the pain and insecurity of losing the love of his life and his identity as an athlete. Stefanie hid her insecurity about her looks and self-worth under several layers of Maybelline, a short skirt, and a near-toxic cloud of body mist.

The kicker is . . . the "us" we wanted others to like wasn't really "us" at all, and the fact that they *didn't* like us wasn't all that surprising, because honestly, we didn't really like "us" either.

Though we were coming from different places of hurt, we had both—like the phantom—bought into the toxic thought that we weren't good enough.

THE MASKS WE WEAR

If you've ever been trick-or-treating as a kid, you know there is a wide variety of masks available. Walk into any Party City or Halloween pop-up store and there are aisles (yes, multiple) of masks to choose from. Scary, fun, superhuman, angelic, demonic—you can be whoever you want, to suit the occasion. Similarly, toxic thoughts can cause us to find masks that serve us for the season we are in.

Masks show up in people's lives in different ways and for specific purposes, and they do serve us for a time. They help us cope with or survive through the various experiences we face. *Coping* is any action we take to deal with the toxic thoughts we believe.[1]

As we continue considering how and why we put on masks, we encourage you to think about times you might have been wearing a mask. Maybe it was to get you through a bad breakup, that busy season of work, or possibly a tragedy. We all have worn masks at one time or another, or even continually. In any case, the goal is to help you understand when you've put them on and allow you the courage to take off any mask that is no longer serving you. Let's dive in by considering the reasons we may hide behind a mask.

Masks for Protection

One reason that people wear masks is to survive in certain situations. We can use masks to protect ourselves from things in our environment that we believe have the potential to hurt us, or we can use them to help us make it through a particularly difficult season.

Maybe the threat to us is a dangerous neighborhood or combative parents. It also can take the form of harsh words spoken over us. You might have heard people say, "You're too fat" or "You don't know how to have fun" or "You're a prude," or maybe even "You are way too loud." These words can bounce around our brain like pinballs, causing us to reevaluate our situation. We may act in a way that is an attempt to prove that statement false, or we might even attempt to prove that it's true.

For some people, a protective mask might take the form of a tough persona. The hardened exterior might protect them from getting beaten up, or worse, killed. It enables them to survive in their environment. The problem is, when this mask that is meant for a specific season is worn into a different time and place, it becomes outdated and even harmful.

We may also put on a protective mask when a romantic relationship goes wrong. Past experiences may have shown us that when we put our heart out there, it can be crushed. People who have been hurt in their dating life might say to themselves, *If I open up to Steve, he will just leave like John did.* Or they might think, *Brie just told me that she loved me. The last time someone told me this, I found out they were cheating on me. It's time to leave.* The past pain and toxic thoughts trigger them to wear a mask that will protect them from further harm.

Think of your heart as a priceless artwork, created by the world's greatest artist. It is placed in the best spot in the museum for all to see. Captivated by its beauty, one visitor asks questions about it, all the while moving closer and closer to the piece. But like any priceless item, it is protected by an alarm. You see, in the past, someone had stolen the art, treated it poorly, and hidden it away until the museum found it again years later. Now, when an admirer gets close enough, the alarm is triggered and the gates close on the room. The museum staff immediately lock the treasure away. Now it is safe, but no one can see its beauty.

Such a story is familiar to those who watch shows like *White Collar* or *The Rookie*, and it's a similar tale for the way people treat their hearts. Your heart is more valuable than any priceless artwork ever could be. It is what connects you to God and to others, and it is your means of experiencing life. When your heart faces potential harm, it is easy to run to a temporary safe place. But if it becomes a permanent place, you lose out on better opportunities for healing and living. A survival mask may serve you for a time, but it will never lead you to the deepest longings of your heart.

One of our clients, Steve, had a hard time dealing with the pain and hurt from his past. There had been several instances at school or church when he had been made fun of for how he looked and carried himself. The words "creep" and "weirdo" echoed through the halls of his heart for years. The toxic thoughts of *I am worthless* and *I am unlovable* became the core of his new identity.

To protect himself, Steve began to make himself scarce. When he went to school, he'd hang out by himself, learning not to engage with other students because that would lead to name-calling and heartbreak. This pattern continued into his adult life, when he poured himself into his work. Eventually, he worked from home, which made him feel even more left out and alone. The mask that had given some relief from others had also caused him to become lonelier and feel stuck in life, with no hope of ever being able to move forward.

With our help, Steve has been able to identify the toxic thoughts he was believing, the masks he had been wearing in different seasons, and how he had been using them to cope. He is now retraining his mind to believe the truth about himself—but more on that later.

Masks for Identity

Another way we put on masks is in the form of a new identity. We do this to trick people into believing we are something we're not—like Caleb pretending to be a party boy to impress a girl, or Stefanie trying to be the kind of girl Ethan liked.

Perhaps a person gets rejected, so they reinvent themselves into someone they think would attract the person they are crushing on. Often, they think, *If I just look more like Tiffany does, then Cade will like me.* They change how they dress, how they act, what they are interested in (or pretend to be interested in) hoping to be liked.

If Tiffany is on the cheer team and dresses in short skirts and tube tops, then they try out for cheer and buy short skirts and tube tops . . . even if they only wore pants before, and short skirts are appalling to them. If they get compliments, it fuels the idea of being more and more like this new persona and less and less like themselves.

One problem with wearing a mask this way is that when the person you are fixated on moves on, you are left with a person (you) that you don't recognize and that you don't like at all. And you are stuck with choosing between this "new you" and the pain from your past. Most people just roll with the "new you," since the pain is too much to bear. This leads to more issues and unproductive behaviors as they seek to escape the pain.

It's as if they reject a part of themselves that caused a specific hurt in their life. Instead of believing the truth, they change who they are and create a mask they think will make them feel better in the here and now.

Masks for Acceptance

Another way this can happen is when someone decides to go against their core beliefs and values in order to be someone that others will like. Some decide that they need to drop their boundaries to please another person. A woman may think, *Josh has been acting disinterested since we had that talk about my boundaries. I better start giving it up to him to keep him around.* She then does things she never thought she would.

The guy has been telling her that he thinks boundaries are silly and he wants to show his love to her in a new way. He promises a new level of intimacy. Sadly, after those boundaries are broken, the guy often leaves soon after. The fun is gone, the excitement fulfilled in the moment.

Promises of greater love and intimacy seem like fairy tales of old, and the woman is left with the broken pieces of the mask she was wearing and the pain of new wounds from compromising her core values.

This also could happen for a person whose girlfriend wants them to look like her favorite celebrity. The girlfriend always makes comments about wanting him to be more buff, to dye his hair a different color, and to wear contacts for a different eye color. She even seems to want him to change parts of his personality to fit what she likes. He makes all of these changes to gain her approval, make her happy, and keep her around. He loses all sense of his own identity, rejecting who he was created to be for a false version. Then that girlfriend breaks up with him, and he is left as a shell of who he used to be. He brings that pain and this new identity into his next relationship, repeating the same cycle over and over.

CONTROLLING OUR PAIN WITH COPING MECHANISMS

As we said earlier, masks are a way of coping with difficult circumstances. We all cope with the things that happen to us in different ways. When we refer to "coping" throughout this book, we are talking about actions people take to be able to deal with the toxic thoughts they believe. In addition to masks, we turn to *coping mechanisms* to help us get through each hardship that we face.

The dictionary definition of a coping mechanism is "an adaptation to environmental stress that is based on conscious or unconscious choice and that enhances control over behavior or gives psychological comfort."[2] Basically, either consciously or subconsciously, we deal with our pain and toxic thoughts by doing things that distract us or help us control our situation.

Hargrave describes some common types of coping in this way:

In response to this primary emotional distress, the individual reacts or copes by extreme fight-or-flight responses. In response to lack of love and loss of identity, the individual may go to one extreme of blame/rage during which he or she expresses aggressive and angry behavior. . . . In response to lack of trustworthiness or safety, the individual may feel compelled to take on control of every situation to the point of being nondependent on others.[3]

Here are some other common ways people attempt to cope with toxic thoughts and pain:

Hurt others

Self-harm

Withdraw

Yell

Use mean words

Hide

Self-sabotage

Turn to distractions/
   obsessions/addictions

Shut themselves off from
   God and others

Over-/undereat

Over-/undersleep

Develop a bitter, negative
   attitude

Over-/underspend

Gossip/slander

Blame/shame

Treat others like objects

Compromise values

Act like nothing bothers
   them

Care about nothing

Try to become the very best

Prove their worth by striving

Over-/underwork

Exhibit perfectionism

Say yes to everything

Say no to everything

Be there for everyone

Overserve

Try to prove how "kind"
   they are

Look at this list. Do any of these behaviors resonate with you? Some of them are not bad in and of themselves. The problem is that they aren't long-term solutions to the real problem. The core issue is the toxic thoughts we believe about ourselves, others, or God. Reacting by coping in these ways can reinforce the toxic thoughts and make them feel even more true. These coping mechanisms can serve us for a time to numb the pain or help us to feel "good enough," but we will keep needing more in order to feel full again.

Coping mechanisms can take a variety of forms. It might be an eating habit that you take on after your boyfriend breaks up with you. When you think about him, you run to the freezer, grab that tub of rocky road, and binge-watch *Riverdale* until you pass out. Or it might be working out—you get stressed from work or from your hectic home life, so you find a form of exercise to help you escape. Coping mechanisms can take seemingly healthy forms (like working out) or unhealthy forms (eating tubs of ice cream or not eating at all).

CALEB'S STORY: VIDEO HERO

I told you about the three dominoes that fell in my life—the end of my dream to play professional basketball, my grandpa passing away, and my long-term girlfriend breaking up with me—leading me to believe the toxic thoughts *God is holding out on me*, *I'm a failure*, and *No one will care about me*. Not only were the circumstances themselves painful but the new toxic beliefs I was holding on to were just as hurtful. There's no way to have such intense beliefs about your core identity and not have that cause a reaction inside of you. To cope with my own toxic thoughts, I began distracting myself and withdrawing from the world.

I dove into video games to run away from the pain in my heart and head. I so desperately wanted to be a hero, if not in the real world, then in a fantasy world.

One day an ad came up for an online game called *World of Warcraft*. It spoke of quests I could take on, epic adventures I could escape to, and prizes I could win. I signed up and this was the start of a massive video game addiction that plagued me for years.

All addiction is based on good desires that we try to meet in unhealthy ways. The core desires to feel important, to feel like I had purpose in life, to make an impact—those things are good. Each time I won a battle, each time I received a new piece of gear for the game, it triggered a little reward in my brain: *Look! You're good enough! You're a winner!*

It seemed harmless, since there wasn't any sex, nudity, or cussing, but it was the addiction to another life that took hold in my heart. I could be anyone I wanted to be, and at least in that world, my heart couldn't be vulnerable enough to be broken or taken advantage of. I might be a failure in this world, but I could be important in another world.

I would spend hours on the game, forgoing healthy living and eating habits. I soon became one of the very best at it. People would invite me to different adventures with them, and I could be a big part of their successes. This only fueled the fire of distraction and helped me to forget my pain and toxic thoughts and the longing I had for something more.

Not everything was negative about this experience. I met some really great people and made an amazing friend (Jordan) who I still talk with to this day. (He even named his kid after me!) There were times that I still talk about with my friends—solving a puzzle or accomplishing something in a game that was very hard to do.

The problem is that when we cope with our pain in ways that lead us away from God and away from taking care of ourselves, we begin to lose big parts of who we are. The toxic thought that led us to cope in the way we are coping can be reinforced even more. For example, real-life opportunities didn't pop up often because so much of my time was spent in the game, which meant the toxic thought *God is holding out on me* kept growing more real. And many areas of my life weren't going so great because of where I was putting my time and energy, which reinforced the toxic thought *I am a failure*.

What was meant to hide my toxic thoughts and keep me from remembering my heartbreak became an all-consuming addiction. I needed to spend more and more time in the game world to continue to be the best. There was always a new version coming out or a new set of gear to find, and a little piece of my core desire to be a "hero" was quenched. But not fully, and I could never get enough.

THE UPSIDE OF COPING

Coping with pain can also bring many positives to your life. Countless stories throughout human existence show the resilience of humans in the face of harsh realities in our broken world.

One of Caleb's favorite athletes is Ray Lewis, who was a middle linebacker for the Baltimore Ravens. Ray won the Super Bowl with the Ravens and was the second linebacker ever to win the Super Bowl MVP award. He also was inducted into the Pro Football Hall of Fame the first year he was eligible, which is an amazing honor.

Ray grew up in a very hard situation at home. His mother, a single parent, would oftentimes be in abusive relationships. Ray found it harder and harder to watch his mother go through this pain. One day he asked his mother for a deck of cards. She replied that there would not be any gambling in her house.

But he wanted to use those cards, not to gamble, but as a tool to get stronger. He would shuffle the deck, then flip over a card. Whatever number was on the card was the number of push-ups he would do. He became stronger and stronger, until he could defend his mother.[4] Ray also began to take part in sports and eventually made his way into the NFL.

Ray could have believed the toxic thought *I'm never going to be safe*. His experiences certainly supported this. But instead, he did something about it. He got strong so that he could secure safety and ensure a better life for himself and his mother.

But his strength couldn't protect him from everything. He learned to find his worth in Christ and not just in his own ability. Ray has submitted the pain and hurt in his life to Jesus, and he loves helping others do the same.

Depending on how you've coped with your pain, it may have brought wonderful results into your life. Some people have amazing careers because they've overworked all their lives to hide the toxic thought *I'm not good enough*. Working hard is something that God wants us all to do. But when we do it out of a need to prove ourselves instead of our desire to love Him, we can feel empty inside.

Coping can also keep us stagnant or can even take us down a path that leads to further problems. In Caleb's case, it kept him stuck and even caused pain in our marriage when he neglected the important things around him. When

Coping serves us for a time, but maybe it's time to find a better way.

Stefanie ran to social media for validation, it took her away from her larger calling and purpose and put her under pressure to be perfect instead of being present and content.

If we are coping with pain to try to cover a toxic thought, whether in a positive or negative way, one day our own strength might give out. Coping serves us for a time, just like masks, to help us deal with our pain. But maybe it's time to find a better way.

ACCENTUATE THE POSITIVE

Is it bad to play video games, put on makeup, or work out? Of course not. It's the *reason* we are driven to these actions that can be detrimental. If we look to anything external to find validation and disprove toxic thoughts, at one point or another, it's going to fail.

Take social media for example. With the rise of platforms like Facebook, Instagram, TikTok, and Snapchat, not only can we control what our lives look like to others, we can also control what *we* look like.

Enhancing your appearance isn't necessarily harmful. The intention behind it is what matters. If the purpose is to hide a toxic thought, it won't get rid of the deeper problem.

Changing the way we look can become an addiction we cling to in an attempt to heal toxic thoughts. But if we are using filters to mask a deeper wound, it can potentially make the feelings of being *not good enough* worse in the long-term.

Several hundred million users across the world are now locked in and active on all social media platforms. People are posting the highlights of their lives: an amazing vacation, a brand-new house, a new baby, and the list goes on.

One toxic thought drives many lives: *Everyone else has it better than me.* We begin to believe that small voice telling us that we are missing out and that we are not good enough. Women see other women in unobtainable shapes and sizes getting thousands of likes and follows. They begin to believe they need to look like these "perfect models." Self-esteem drops through the floor, and they look for ways to stack up to the demands of society.

When you record a video on Instagram, for instance, a filter menu pops up. Some options give you a cat's ears and nose. Others make your eyes twice as big. Still others change pretty much everything about you—even your complexion and the color of your hair.

There's even one called "the no-filter filter." You would think this means all-natural, as in, "We're not changing a thing," right? Wrong! I (Stefanie) tried it once and it blurred my skin so much it looked like I didn't have a nose anymore. There was nothing natural about it!

Granted, sometimes filters are good. There are times we need to filter ourselves to avoid hurting someone else. We might filter our language, for example, to avoid offending someone. You might avoid bringing up your dinner at Outback Steakhouse around your friend, the vegan animal rights activist. We might even filter out topics we know will be painful for some people. For instance, if your friend's grandmother has just passed away, you might avoid talking about the amazing time you just had with your own grandma or grandpa. Having discernment in communication is vital.

So, are filters that change the way we look online bad? We've come to realize that these filters are a mask for many people. Just as with Caleb's video gaming, filters and social media personas can be very addictive. The toxic beliefs of *I'm not lovable* and *I'm worthless* can temporarily feel better when the likes, DMs, and attention come rolling in.

STEFANIE'S STORY: "PINCH ME"

Recently I had a "pinch me" type of moment. I'd been using the YouVersion Bible app on my phone almost every day for about thirteen years. Perhaps you have used this app. There are reading plans for any stage of life.

I used to follow a "read the Bible in a year" plan, and I would complete it each year and start over again. I could read it or I could listen to it on my way to work, on hikes, and while doing things around the house. Recently they began a series called "Verse of the Day," where different notable pastors, speakers, artists, and singers share the daily verse and some short thoughts about it. I was thrilled when they asked me, of all people, to share the verse of the day. For someone who loves getting to share about Jesus with others, it was a dream come true!

I prayed for days about what I was going to say, and then I got ready to film. I did my usual hair and makeup and then recorded my video. I thought I had done a pretty good job, but when I played it back, I was shocked. I looked so pale and puffy. I looked . . . *terrible*.

How could this be? I'd seen myself on screen hundreds of times on Instagram, and I'd never had this problem. Then it dawned on me. *Filters.* Every time I posted on Instagram, I tried out a new filter. My go-to was the "honey" filter, which evened out my skin tone and added more color. I thought it improved my overall appearance.

But this wasn't Instagram. I was just filming myself straight on my 4K-quality camera, with no filter. And I didn't like what I was seeing. I could have cried. In fact, I did. Not because of the way I looked, but because of the way I felt. Who was I to share my thoughts about Jesus' love with others when I couldn't even get past my own insecurities? I felt completely unqualified.

The worst part was, I thought I was beyond that. I wasn't an insecure little teenager hiding behind layers of makeup anymore. *Jesus*, I prayed, *didn't we already get over this hurdle of insecurity? Why am I going back to my old ways?*

As I sat there crying, Jesus whispered His sweet words of love over me. *You are loved. I will help you.* Then Caleb came in and showered me with his own sweet words of encouragement. "You look stunning, my love," he said. "I'm so proud of you."

The funny thing is, the people at YouVersion asked me to reshoot that video because they wanted it all done in one cut instead of multiple cuts as I had done.

But I was glad.

Caleb and I vowed that we would not use filters anymore on Instagram—not because it was inherently wrong, but because I wanted to see myself the way God sees me. And that's what I wanted others to see too. I am made in God's image. We all are.

Without even realizing it was happening, I had gotten so used to the filtered, masked version of me that when I saw myself without the filter, I didn't like who I saw.

The next video I submitted was more authentic. I was less concerned with how I looked and more focused on who God wanted to speak to through me. My posture had changed from self-serving (*How do I look?*) to serving others (*How are others seeing themselves as a result of what I'm sharing?*).

It's been over a year since I stopped using filters, and a lot has changed. I have become less dependent on how others see me. I have recorded my face a lot less and focused on God and others a lot more. I have become more attuned to the long-term vision God has for my life. And I keep asking Him to show me how He sees me and others—not through a filter, but through His lens of love.

The more dependent we are on our masks, the further away we drift from ourselves, others, and God.

That's the point. The more dependent we become on our masks (and/or false personas) the further away we drift from our true selves, the people we care about, and God. The goal of relationships is to draw people closer to us. Putting on a mask or false persona actually pushes others further away from who we really are. If we don't learn to accept and embrace who we are in God's eyes, we will always be a shell of what He wants us to be.

This might seem weird, but maybe you need to thank yourself and God for giving you a mask to wear and ways to cope. Perhaps what you have been through was so rough that you needed a mask to survive. We encourage you to take a deep breath and thank God for the ways He has helped you get from one day to the next. And now He's led you here. Though the masks and old ways of coping got you through your last season, they may not serve you well in the next one.

I had been wearing masks for so long, trying to get guys to validate me. I finally made a big shift that I'll share more about in the pages to come. It allowed me to have no mask when I met Caleb, and he got to see the real me. That's who he fell in love with, and it was so freeing.

Friend, we know you might feel exhausted right now by the masks you've had to wear and the ways you've found to cope with your pain. But we also know there's so much freedom for you ahead. You are a masterpiece. We get why you locked up the beautiful painting—your heart—but we would love to show you how to unlock it in a safe way.

CONNECTIVITY VERSUS COMMUNITY

How much time do you spend scrolling on your phone each day? Each week? Is it helping you feel more loved? More known? More seen? What about people you see in person? Do you feel known by them? Heard by them? Do they feel seen by you?

Research has shown that the more time people scroll online, the more alone they feel.[5] Never before in human history have we been so accessible to so many people. But is all the accessibility making us put on even more masks?

I (Stefanie) rearranged the pillows on the couch so I could lean back. I settled into my comfy spot, opened my favorite social media app, and started scrolling, writing comment after comment on friends' posts to encourage and support them. I felt myself get more and more anxious. When my thumbs started hurting, I realized I had spent over an hour watching highlight reels of people I had never met in person. During that time, a dear friend had called, and I let her call go to voicemail. I had work to do—this was a lot of work after all.

I spent over an hour "connecting" with others. But why did I feel so alone? Why did I feel so unseen? I then shared several things on my own Instagram page, thinking I'd feel less alone. Instead, I felt more anxious. Why, when I had more people talking to me than ever before, did I feel so empty? Something had to change.

It seems we have substituted quantity for quality. We may have a thousand Facebook friends but still feel invisible. We may be in tons of online groups, yet wonder if anyone really knows us.

It doesn't have to be just online. Where in your life are you substituting surface-level interaction for true heart intimacy? Those moments when you're faced with choosing between being your true self and putting on a mask? Using a survival mask has probably proved valuable in some social situations, but is it still serving you well in all situations today? Discernment is still important for guarding your heart, but what about those wonderful, glorious moments when the mask is off, and you are met with total love, community, and kindness even from a stranger who might turn into a friend?

What if you could slow down when talking with others? What if you met the basic question "How are you doing?" with honesty, and your reply was received with listening and caring ears? As you learn more about the toxic thoughts and coping mechanisms that have been holding you back, you will find true healing from past experiences and be able to find those close relationships you long for. You will experience wholehearted love as God intended.

MAKING IT PERSONAL

Scripture to Apply

Feel free to read the following verses and note what they say about how God created you and how He values you as His creation. Summarize what you see in these verses in the space provided below.

> You created my inmost being; you knit me together in my mother's womb. I praise you because I am fearfully and wonderfully made; your works are wonderful, I know that full well. (Psalm 139:13-14)

> Let the king be enthralled by your beauty; honor him, for he is your lord. (Psalm 45:11)

> I tell you, do not worry about your life, what you will eat or drink; or about your body, what you will wear. Is not life more than food, and the body more than clothes? (Matthew 6:25)

As God's chosen people, holy and dearly loved, clothe yourselves with compassion, kindness, humility, gentleness and patience. (Colossians 3:12)

Keep me as the apple of your eye; hide me in the shadow of your wings. (Psalm 17:8)

Questions to Consider

1. What are some ways that you have been coping with toxic thoughts? Look at the list on page 57 for possible ideas.

2. Is there a mask you've been putting on that is no longer serving you? Describe it below.

Call to Action

Write down one of the verses above on a Post-it Note and put it on your mirror. Each time you look in the mirror, remind yourself of God's truth over your life.

Pray this prayer today:

Lord, please fill all my empty places.[6] Fill my heart with Your amazing, lavish love. Let me get my worth from You. Let me believe Your words about myself, others, and my circumstances today. Please let me know the truth about who You say that I am. Help me not to cope in negative ways that are hurting me. Thank You that You have a new path for me filled with hope, joy, and peace. Amen.

Stuck in a Cycle

RECOGNIZING THE LIES
THAT ROB YOU OF FREEDOM

CALEB'S STORY: SWEET REVENGE?

"You'll never be good enough to play college basketball."

The words echoed in my heart and soul, straight to my core. *I'm not good enough, and I never will be.* I stared down at the messy old wooden desk covered with students' files. The dusty air was the perfect backdrop for words that went deep enough to kill dreams.

My high school guidance counselor, himself a former college football player, looked back at me with a piercing, immovable gaze as he told me that what I had always worked for would never happen, no matter how hard I tried.

I left his office, despondent, head down, eyes glazed over. I had come in with excitement for the future, a great basketball season behind me. I had decided to seek my counselor's guidance, given that he had coached and played at my dream school, albeit a different sport. I thought he could still give me pointers.

Instead, his statement was etched on my heart like a tombstone. As I sat with those words for a few weeks, I couldn't shake the feeling that what I wanted most in the world was to prove I *was* good enough.

So I worked twice as hard and spent countless hours in the gym. At home, I practically lived at the basketball hoop on the street corner. Morning, evening, it didn't matter. I practiced every moment I could. Each shot was aimed at my counselor. Each basket, proof that I *could* be good enough.

Three years later, as I stared down at the scholarship offer to play at my dream school, those words *I'm not good enough*—now almost an anthem for me—finally felt like they might not be true. My worth and effort had gone completely into this endeavor, my whole life invested in this one thing. I felt like I finally had power over that toxic thought, thanks to my hard work.

I even got my revenge tale. Like the scene in *Pretty Woman* (yes, I'm comparing myself to Julia Roberts), I saw my old counselor again on my college campus one day. He had gotten a full-time coaching position at the university. I was wearing my new team basketball hoodie, the kind that only a team member would have, and when I happened to see my counselor walking toward me, I stood up nice and tall and said, "Big mistake, HUGE!"

Well, not really. But I looked him in the eye, puffing out my chest like a gladiator after a massive victory at the Colosseum, and said, "Hey, Mr. Smith, so nice to see you."

I made sure the basketball logo on my jacket was uncovered. I didn't want him to miss it. He might not have even remembered that conversation years ago, but none of that mattered. I felt like I had conquered my foe. I was now good enough. Or so it seemed . . .

For years, I had coped with this feeling of not being good enough by overcompensating on the basketball court. I was putting all my eggs in one basket, so to speak, which any player serious about going all the way should do.

If you remember the story of losing my sports career to an injury my senior year of college, you can see now why that was so devastating. Since my worth was fully based in basketball, in being good enough, losing out on that dream sent me down a path of coping in ways I never imagined.

Drinking, partying, becoming addicted to pornography, being overinvolved in video games, and even pushing physical boundaries in relationships—I was trying to find a way to be *good enough* again. Those moments where I compromised, in ways I had prided myself on never doing before, only perpetuated the feeling of *not* being good enough again, and again, and again.

I thought I had done it. I thought I had conquered that feeling, but I was now experiencing it on a whole new level. I was stuck in a cycle, believing toxic thoughts to my core, and I couldn't get out.

A VICIOUS CYCLE

Have you experienced this? Has someone spoken hurtful words over you that you believed? Have you coped in ways you wish you hadn't? Have you felt stuck in a crazy cycle and not known why?

The thing is, believing toxic thoughts can happen to anyone, and as you learned in chapter 3, they can cause you to cope in harmful ways and keep you from the kinds of relationships you dream of. But when you find healing from past pain or trauma, you can experience wholehearted love as God intended.

So far in this healing process, you've come to understand the reasons that you want wholehearted love, and you've identified the kind of love you are looking for. You've also begun to uncover the toxic thoughts you might be believing about yourself, and you've considered the ways you might be coping with those thoughts.

Now it's time to look at how those thoughts and coping mechanisms can lead to vicious cycles that end in destruction, confusion, and hurt. We like to call them "toxic cycles."

THE TIP OF THE ICEBERG

Titanic. It's an epic tale, a true story, about a massive ship that sank in the Atlantic Ocean in 1912. People believed that it was so big, so massive, that nothing could get in its way, nothing could ever sink it.

But on its maiden voyage it struck an iceberg and sank. That's the trouble with icebergs. Most of what exists is beneath the surface. And what's beneath the surface can bring down even the most indestructible ship ever created.

Toxic thoughts are a lot like icebergs. They are not surface level. They go far beneath the surface to our core. They are deep enough and strong enough to take us down, along with those around us. We can't see them, but they have a huge effect on every part of our lives.

As we talked about in chapter 2, toxic thoughts are hurtful and inaccurate things we believe about our identity—*unloved, unworthy, voiceless, alone,* and many more. When we feel this way, it causes something to happen inside of us. Our bodies and minds can't just sit with those thoughts; we have to respond. This leads us to cope in specific ways. In the last chapter we talked about some of the ways people cope with their toxic thoughts. They may withdraw, yell, blame, or self-sabotage, for example.

We also talked about the fact that our brain creates specific paths based on the way we cope after a toxic thought is triggered. Our brain will follow these trails on autopilot unless we do something to stop them.

A *toxic cycle* is when your toxic thought leads to a coping mechanism, which reinforces your toxic thought (or another toxic thought), which then leads you to the same or another coping mechanism. This cycle continues automatically, over and over again.[1]

Imagine a little girl named Sarah, growing up in an abusive household. Yelling and screaming were the background music to her evenings at home. Her father and mother blamed her for their troubles, saying they wished she were different or that they had never had her. She began to believe the toxic thoughts *I am a mistake, I never should have been born,* and *I am unloved.* And do you blame her? She also felt unloved if she didn't do everything well, so she coped by trying to act perfect. She thought, *If I act perfect in every way, I will be loved and I will prove myself.*

No one is perfect. It's completely natural that Sarah would eventually mess up and then feel like a failure. This triggered her to believe she was a mistake, so to cope she followed her parents' example and blamed someone else.

Sarah eventually grows up, moves out of the house, and gets a job. She is good at her job. After all, she is a perfectionist. But one day, Sarah makes a mistake, and the boss brings her into her office and says she needs to do better. Sarah quietly takes the reprimand, then goes back to her desk. But when a coworker later asks for her help on a project, Sarah blows up. She yells at the coworker and blames him for the mistake she made earlier.

Hargrave explains blaming reactionary behavior like this:

> People who are self-reactive with blame feel that they are deeply entitled to be loved and act on the violation in an accusatory fashion. We can imagine that when they feel this lack of identity, they ask themselves, "Why was I not loved?" The driving force of the fight reaction

indicates that they were not loved because the others in relationship with them were evil, incompetent, self-focused, or simply ignorant to what they were supposed to provide. In response to the lack of identity, blamers tend to demand or demean others to try to secure the identity and proper sense of self.[2]

As you can see, Sarah's toxic cycle had an impact on her life, and her learned coping behavior based on the toxic thought she believed was negatively impacting the relationships she had at work.

You have probably seen this play out in your own relationships when your toxic thoughts are triggered. Understanding your triggers allows you to spot when they are being activated and gives you a chance to stop your reactions in their tracks and keep them from spiraling out of control.

Understanding your triggers allows you to stop your reactions in their tracks.

One of the most freeing feelings we can have is understanding that we are not crazy for reacting in a specific way. When we look at what triggered certain coping mechanisms, we see that the toxic thought had to go somewhere. No wonder so many people respond to seemingly small irritations with such intense reactions. Just like the iceberg, an issue can seem insignificant from surface level. But when we look deeper, it makes sense that a seemingly small thing could sink us.

TOXIC CYCLES COLLIDE

In a relationship, one of the hardest things that happens is when two people's toxic thoughts and cycles are being triggered and are triggering one another's at the same time. This can easily happen in an argument, or even in conversation, and it is referred to as toxic cycles *colliding.*

It happens like this: A toxic thought is triggered in Person A. Person A then goes directly to their coping mechanism. Person A's coping mechanism triggers Person B's toxic thoughts. Person B's toxic thoughts cause them to react with a coping mechanism, which then reinforces Person A's toxic thought, making it seem true. Person A copes again, reinforcing Person B's toxic thought. This cycle continues like a nonstop seesaw, although much less fun.

Toxic thoughts can collide in any relationship. A collision can be triggered in romantic relationships, in friendships, in family relationships, at work, online, at the grocery store, while driving, and anywhere else. The toxic cycle can even impact how we interact with God and how we see ourselves.

Let's talk about Sarah again.

Imagine she starts dating a guy named Fred. When Fred was growing up, he had a difficult time reading. He got some negative messages from classmates and teachers, so he believed the toxic thoughts *I'm not capable* and *I'm not good enough.* One of the ways Fred copes is by overworking, not asking for help, and trying to prove himself. When Fred's efforts aren't what he sees as *good enough,* he withdraws from others and from God.

Now Fred and Sarah spark up a romantic relationship. Sarah feels loved by Fred because he's constantly telling her how beautiful she is. Fred loves that Sarah compliments his work and tells him how smart he is.

But stressors occur in both Sarah's and Fred's lives. One day, Sarah comes home from the bad day at work we talked about earlier. Her toxic thought of being a mistake had triggered her to cope by yelling and blaming another employee. The employee (who had been a friend of Sarah's) acted cold and heartless in response. This reinforced Sarah's feeling of being unloved.

When Sarah pulls into the driveway, she sees that all the other trash cans in her neighborhood are out on the street. Her trash can isn't, even though she had reminded Fred about it that morning. *Fred doesn't love me,* she thinks. The first thing she says when she walks into the house is, "Fred, did you take the trash out?"

Her tone is mean, frustrated, and cold. Fred has had a busy workday and has totally forgotten about the garbage. "No," he says sheepishly.

Sarah responds, "You are so lazy! You never take care of anything!"

Fred's toxic thoughts of *I'm not capable, I'm not good enough* are triggered big-time. His coping mechanism of trying to prove himself kicks in. He tells Sarah how hard he worked all day, all the projects he accomplished, and the other things he has done to help around the house.

This triggers Sarah to feel unloved, unimportant, and unseen (since she had reminded Fred about the trash). His forgetfulness feels like confirmation that he doesn't love her. His defending himself and not taking responsibility makes her feel even more unseen. She yells, "You never listen to me. Why don't you care about me?"

Fred angrily leaves the room and slams the door behind him. He withdraws from Sarah and the situation, which only proves to her that she isn't good enough to be loved.

Fred and Sarah were both desiring connection. They were desiring to be seen, known, and loved by the people they care most about. They both had difficult days and needed the other person's love. The series of events and the exchanges between the two of them reinforced their toxic thoughts. Their coping mechanisms reinforced the toxic thoughts even more. They felt unseen, unloved, unappreciated, disrespected, and unknown.

The way Sarah's and Fred's toxic cycles collided is what happens so often in relationships. As you can see, they both were drawing from their own painful experiences and then spewing their pain on the other person.

As Hargrave says, it is not so much that individuals are "choosing relationships that mimic unresolved issues or unprocessed behavior in past relationships (i.e., a man marries a woman just like his mother or ex-wife), but that current relationships simply tend to bring out our unresolved and painful issues."[3]

This cycle is where a lot of marriages and relationships get stuck. In a dating relationship, it becomes hard to build and sustain a connection after one or multiple collisions like this. Sometimes, this is the place a relationship ends, and both people leave feeling frustrated and unloved, with deeper wounds than they started with. This new experience only reinforces how they already felt about themselves to their core. For married couples, it can become a very unhappy and isolated place to be if they stay in their toxic cycles, continuing to trigger each other day in and day out. It can be a toxic environment to live in.

Reinforcing each other's toxic thoughts and coping mechanisms is a vicious cycle. Both people might have started to take off their masks with the other person. But the pain causes them to place them back on again. They may begin to pour their energy into other things besides the relationship—anywhere they can feel safer. The colliding cycles can also keep them from growing in a particular area—almost like a time machine that freezes their growth.

Can you relate to Sarah and Fred? Have you ever been in a relationship that seemed so amazing, but then suddenly deteriorated? You are left confused, frustrated, and brokenhearted.

A LITTLE TRUTH MIXED IN

A dear client, Kari, grew up in the foster care system. Needless to say, her home life was extremely unstable, many of the people who came into her life were not safe for her to be around, and she rarely stayed with the same family for long. Abandonment became familiar and, eventually, the norm. *Maybe it's me,* she thought. *Maybe I'm the reason people always leave. Maybe I'm a mistake. Maybe I'm toxic. Maybe I should always be alone.*

Fast-forward to her adult years. Kari attached quickly to people she dated. Her coping mechanism was to instantly trust anyone who showed interest. *If I hold them very close, do everything with them, and show them how much I care, maybe they won't leave.*

Kari asked to meet her boyfriends' families right away. She loved feeling connected and being a part of a family, and she put on blinders to any red flags. She was so desperate for connection that she stayed in unhealthy relationships much longer than was good for her.

She did everything for her love interests and their families. She bought them many presents (even if it meant opening up another credit card). She made them meals, took them out to dinner, and helped them pay their rent or make a car payment.

Her mask was everything for everyone that she cared about. She always said yes. She always showed up. She never said no. It didn't matter if it crossed her boundaries physically, emotionally, spiritually, or financially. She didn't know who she really was, and she was drained in every way. But if that meant people would love her and stay, it was worth it.

Unfortunately, people didn't stay. In relationship after relationship, she was used, abused, and dropped. Cheated on, taken advantage of, and left trying to pick up the pieces of her broken heart, her empty wallet, and her deteriorating health. She chalked it up to the fact that either she must *attract* the worst people in the world or she must *be* the worst person in the world.

As you can see, there are many reasons that toxic cycles can feel frustrating and confusing. As we've shared previously, toxic thoughts stem from an area of pain and/or a violation of love and trust. But they are grounded in a little bit of truth mixed with a lot of lies. It's true that Kari didn't have safe, stable adults to care about her. But why did she believe the toxic thoughts? Why was she continually attracting unsafe people?

THINKING IN EXTREMES

As children, our brains are not developed enough to think rationally about people and circumstances. Instead, *extreme thinking* occurs. That is, we tend to think in black-or-white ways. In a young person's mind, there are no "in-betweens," and they don't understand gray areas. They think either that they are loved by their parents or they are not. This is why they can have extreme reactions to a situation.

What we wish Kari could have understood is this:

My parents are people. They are hurting people who are hurting me out of their own pain. This has nothing to do with me or my identity. It has everything to do with them, and how well they have come to understand their own needs and motivations. I'm not bad. They're not bad. I don't enjoy going from home to home, but it doesn't mean that I'm not good enough. People will leave at times, but that's not a reflection on me. I want to be who I am. I am okay if people leave or go because my worth doesn't change. I want to love others well, in a safe way.

As adults looking at Kari's situation, we would be able to help her understand this. Of course, it is not her fault she didn't have dependable adults. She's not the reason people have not provided stability for her. But based on her level of brain development, little Kari wasn't yet able to think like this.

Instead, she jumped to two extreme conclusions: *I'm the worst little girl in the world* and *My family and these people I'm meeting are the worst people in the world.* People who were supposed to take responsibility for her weren't around. Confusion of responsibility, toxic cycles, and extreme thinking became her norm.

As she had the thought *I'm the worst little girl in the world,* many toxic thoughts and coping mechanisms stemmed from it. One of these was the toxic thought *Everyone will leave me*—grounded in the truth of her own experience—which caused her to attach quickly and intensely to others. People who had extreme toxic thoughts that played off of Kari's were the ones showing her attention. She didn't give herself space or time to find out if they were safe people to attach herself to. Instead, her fear of them leaving caused her to overgive in every way. When a person walked out of her life or treated her badly, her belief that she was the worst person and was always going to be around the worst people was reinforced time and time again.

In the midst of this, Kari struggled with being overweight. One of her coping mechanisms to numb her pain was eating. Food became her safe place. But her weight gain caused her to believe even more toxic thoughts. *I only deserve people who treat me like trash, because I'm fat* was the message she often told herself.

As Kari's coping mechanisms continued to reinforce her toxic thoughts, she became attracted to men who weren't safe. She began to cope in more extreme ways.

RECOGNIZING THE TRUTH

When any of us have toxic thoughts about our body image, there can be elements of truth attached to the lie. We might believe the toxic thought *I'm fat* after stepping on the scale and seeing the numbers go higher than before.

The truth: the numbers on the scale *are* higher.

The truth: numbers on a scale don't increase or decrease my intrinsic worth.

But the message *I'm fat* is what can play like a broken record in our mind.

When we attach words to our core identity in this way, it's very harmful. Instead of taking on the negative identity of *I'm fat and ugly*, we could think, *I gained some extra weight. I only get one body to take care of, and I want to take good care of it.* The latter is a gentler way to talk to ourselves.

We can start to see ourselves as more or less valuable depending on how we see our bodies. And believing we should be treated as "less than" based on this view can prove detrimental for many people. Belittling ourselves just pushes us further into a toxic cycle. It doesn't allow us to give ourselves the respect we deserve.

Our culture can enforce toxic thoughts about body image based on what we see on social media, in magazines, and on TV. It's hard to even recognize the truth when there are so many different sources telling us the toxic thoughts we're believing are true. As much as we'd like to change all these external factors, we can't. We can't control other people, so the place to start is with ourselves.

Becoming aware of what we have control over and what we don't have control over is vital. Many people blame others for things that they could take responsibility for. And many take responsibility for things they shouldn't. Let's look at the definition of *responsibility*:

> *responsibility*: the state or fact of having a duty to deal with something or of having control over someone.[4]

When we take responsibility for the things that are within our control and let go of the things that aren't, it frees us to sort through much confusion and allows us to make healthier choices.

When we take responsibility for things within our control and let go of things that aren't, it frees us to make healthier choices.

The toxic thoughts we believe can feel so true. It can seem like there is so much substance to back them up. It's as if we were lawyers, finding ways to justify the lies. We can point to many things over the course of our lives that appear to prove the lies are true. They are part of us. They are our identity. Toxic cycles confuse us about where the responsibility lies. We are so dizzy from the cycle it's hard to know what is what. How do we know what to take responsibility for and what we can be free to let go?

BREAKING FREE FROM SHAME AND GUILT

Some of the things we are most ashamed of are the coping mechanisms we've used to hide our toxic thoughts. When we act out in a way we wish we hadn't, it is painful. We can have shame over behavior that we are not proud of.

But there's a difference between shame and guilt. Knowing the difference will help you gain freedom to let go of shame from your past.

Shame is feeling that you as a human being are bad.
Guilt is knowing that you did something wrong or bad.

Picture a little girl at the store with her mother, where she sees a candy aisle filled with everything chocolate imaginable. She spots her favorite candy bar, Hershey's chocolate, and asks her mom, "Can I have a Hershey's? Please?"

"No," her mother responds and walks toward the next aisle. Disappointed, the little girl stands there, still eyeing her favorite treat. She waits for her mother to turn the corner, then grabs the bar and sneaks it into her pocket.

Once they get home, she creeps up to her bedroom, rips open the shiny, brown wrapper, and eats the chocolate. When the immediate satisfaction begins to wear off, she feels a rush of emotion. Her conscience is going off like a school bell, and she is left with two choices: respond in shame or respond in guilt.

If the little girl responds in shame, she never confesses what she did. She feels the guilt but chooses to believe the lies *I'm the worst little girl in the world, I'm a mistake, I'm unlovable.* She feels paralyzed by her theft and doesn't tell anyone about it. She hides from others and continues to believe these lies, sinking further and further into her shame. Years later she is still carrying around this burden.

If, on the other hand, she responds in guilt, it means she realizes she has done something wrong and can take responsibility to fix it. She can confess to her mother and ask how to make up for her actions. If her mother receives her with grace, kindness, and love, healing can take place. They can go to the store and pay for the candy. Perhaps the young girl can do a chore to "pay" for it. They can decide together and find a way to make amends. This brings freedom: the thoughts of having done something bad don't have to haunt her.

It is okay that we feel guilty when we do something wrong. We have a conscience for a reason. All of us have sinned and fall short of God's glory, and there's not one human on the planet who has not made a mistake. We all act in evil ways at times, but our guilt doesn't have to be our whole identity. If we know that truth, we can make amends, and we can get better. By bringing our wrongdoing into the open, we feel empowered to do something different in the future. It helps us be free.

But when, out of shame, we take on our mistakes as part of

our identity, it continually spurs us further into actions we aren't proud of. We never gain the freedom of feeling we can do anything different. We don't feel empowered to change.

Instead, we need to replace the shame with truth. Then we need to make repentance a priority, before God, ourselves, and others. If there is something we need to make amends for, we can do that. Then we'll be able to move on in freedom instead of feeling stuck our entire lives.

Knowing that we can make mistakes and that it's okay is so powerful. When you know those mistakes no longer define you, it helps you to walk away from unhealthy decisions and actions in the future. Receiving God's forgiveness and forgiving and being kind to yourself is healing.

HIDING OUR SHAME

Many people have a hard time being in a healthy, long-lasting relationship because they have been hiding an area of shame. They keep their partner at arm's length because they don't want them to learn their secret.

Shame makes us feel alone. And it naturally separates us from our most important relationships. It leads us to cope in more negative ways and can paralyze us from experiencing intimacy.

Let's go back to the little girl who stole the candy bar. If she felt guilty and realized that she could fix the problem, she would be able to make up for her actions. She could be forgiven and empowered, and she could feel free.

If she felt shame, she couldn't fix the problem. She would feel embarrassed and hide. Many times, when we start hiding one part of ourselves, we also hide another part. All the parts that seem less lovable we cover up. This hiding leads us to be less connected to others. Although humans long for connection, shame doesn't allow it.

Connection with others is what gives life purpose and meaning. Anything blocking us from having the connection we desire can also lead to more toxic thoughts and negative coping mechanisms. Shame causes us to fear being disconnected from others If they find us out. We believe the lie *If they know this secret about me, I will no longer be worthy of love and connection.*

The people who have deep, meaningful, wholehearted connections with others are those who have the courage to share who they really are. They are willing to reveal their imperfections and take off their masks.

Our world can teach *perfect = lovable.* But this is unattainable. The truth is, we are saved in our sins. We are loved in our worst moments by the God who created the universe. Nothing you or I have done can ever separate us from the love of God.

> *The people who have wholehearted connections with others are those who have the courage to share who they really are.*

Is there an area of your life you've hidden from others? Can you relate to the little girl stealing the candy bar? Have you ever been stuck in shame? Are you currently feeling shame about something?

Finding a trusted friend or counselor you can confide in is important. Being able to make amends for anything you have done and allowing God to forgive you after you confess your sins sets you free. This sets you up to stop destructive patterns.

Don't be shocked that you've hidden things. You're not alone. People have been hiding from their shame since the beginning of time.

NAKED AND UNASHAMED

You are probably familiar with the story of Adam and Eve and their fall from God's grace. Adam and Eve were naked and unafraid because they were without sin or fault. They had never disobeyed God, and they lived in perfect harmony with Him and one another. But then they disobeyed God, and when He came looking for them, they went into hiding. They had once been naked and unashamed. But suddenly they were so aware of their nakedness.

Eve's pain cycle might have gone something like this:

She had a toxic thought: *God is withholding good from me.*
She used a coping mechanism: trying to convince Adam to
   go away from God.
She put on a "mask."

Adam's response might have happened like this:

He believed Eve's lie: *God is withholding from us.*
He had a toxic thought: *I'm a failure.*
He used coping mechanisms: he hid from God, and he
   blamed Eve.

Their cycles played off of each other's and spurred responses. They hid from God and each other.

As we read this story in Genesis chapter 3, we're curious about some things. What would have happened if Adam and Eve hadn't deflected responsibility? What if Adam had come clean right away after hearing God ask, "Have you eaten of the tree I commanded you not to eat from?"

What if he had said, "Yes God, I did. You told me not to. I am so very sorry. Will You please forgive me? I feel ashamed because I disobeyed You, and I wish I could take it back. I hate being disconnected from You. I hate knowing I am naked. Will You please forgive me, Lord? I should have looked out for my wife. I wish I had spoken the truth to her and reminded her of how good You are to us. I wish I had told her not to listen to the crafty serpent because he is a liar. I should have put my foot down and said, 'We will trust God and obey Him only.'"

What would God have done in response if Adam had immediately taken full responsibility? Do you think He would have forgiven him? Do you think the punishment and Fall would have happened? Would it have been less intense?

We will never know the answers to these questions on this side of heaven, but we do know God loves when we take ownership of our mistakes. The tactic of "but she told me to and she manipulated me" has been tried with God since the beginning. It didn't work then, and it won't work now. He knows everything about our hearts, and He wants us to be honest with Him because He cares so deeply about us not continuing in shame.

And what about when God asked Eve, "What is this you have done?" What if she had said, "I listened to a lie. I believed a toxic thought about You, God. I thought that You were holding out good things from me. I'm sorry I believed that. I should listen to Your voice alone. I know You are so good to me, and I am so sorry for disobeying You. I never want to do that again. Please forgive me."

We see how believing toxic thoughts, not taking responsibility for their actions, and deflecting blame caused pain and deterioration in Adam and Eve's relationships. They felt separated from God and from each other. It's the same for us when we don't take responsibility for our actions and we get stuck in a toxic cycle.

STEFANIE'S STORY: THIRD-GRADE ROBIN HOOD

Everyone gathered around Johnny's desk in our third-grade classroom. I stood on my tiptoes behind a classmate with big, curly red hair so I could see what everyone was looking at. It was the coolest thing I had ever seen! A pen that could draw, but also play sounds and record your voice and play it back. It looked so sophisticated. It was the most beautiful thing I'd ever seen.

This was before most people had cell phones, and even the ones some parents carried only had buttons for making a quick call. This pen was the talk of our third-grade class, and I couldn't wait to rush home and tell my mom I NEEDED one. I went on and on about it and how I wanted one so badly.

She said, "We'll see."

Johnny was a generous classmate. He let many people borrow his pen throughout the next couple of days. But by the end of the week, his pen was gone. On Monday, our teacher announced that the pen had been stolen. She asked us all to be on the lookout for it.

My face felt beet red. I wondered if anyone could tell. But I stayed quiet.

I'd had the best weekend writing notes and recording phrases on that pen. It was SO cool! I needed to use it in secret, so I "played in my room" every chance I got. I thought about bringing it back to Johnny on Monday, but then he would know I had stolen it. Someone asked if I'd seen it, and I said no. The guilt ate away at me all day.

When I got home from school, my mom had a big surprise for me. She had bought me a brand-new pen exactly like Johnny's! I was so excited to have one all my own. But the guilt was still gnawing at me. I contemplated what to do. *Should I come clean? NO, I can't. No one can know what I did. But how can I live with this guilt?*

The next day, Johnny's pen was constantly on my mind. I was outside playing with our next-door neighbors. They only had their mom, and the family was struggling financially at the time. I knew the kids didn't have much, so I brought out Johnny's pen and gave it to Maya. She was ecstatic.

The following day at school, Johnny had a new pen from his parents. Whew . . . I was off the hook! *Johnny is rich, and his parents got him a new pen,* I thought. *Maya is poor, and now she has a cool pen. And I have a brand-new pen that I can bring to school too!*

I rationalized my guilt. I repeated these phrases over and over to make myself feel better. Even all these years later, the shame is still near. I don't know if Johnny will ever read this book, but I hope he does. I want to say I am so sorry for stealing your pen. I am so sorry for lying to you and for the pain and frustration it caused you. I'd also like to apologize to my teacher and classmates. I hope you can forgive me.

It's amazing the way we try to cover our mistakes, how we rationalize our guilt. But it's clear that shame took hold in those moments of my childhood. I tried to present myself as the third-grade Robin Hood, as a good and moral person. But inside I knew I was "bad." I grew a hatred for myself. I went into hiding. I shut off parts of myself that I felt weren't desirable.

Hiding feels safe. It's a way we've coped. But it can't be a place we stay if we want to experience all the goodness God has in store for us. The toxic cycles have been so very painful. But it doesn't have to stay this way. Knowing why they've happened can allow us to feel less crazy. I pray that knowing God has something better will spark hope in your soul.

You are loved beyond measure. God has seen you in your darkest moments, and He hasn't left you—even in the moments that you've wanted to hide the most. He is better than we could ever imagine. He offers redemption for Sarah and Fred. He offers redemption for Kari. He offers redemption for Caleb. He offers redemption for me.

He also offers redemption for *you*. And it's just a couple of pages away.

Scripture to Apply

We encourage you to read the following verses and note what they say about forgiveness and how to live your life in peace with others. Summarize what you see in these verses in the space provided below.

> If we confess our sins, he is faithful and just to forgive
> us our sins and to cleanse us from all unrighteousness.
> (1 John 1:9, ESV)

> Let all bitterness and wrath and anger and clamor
> and slander be put away from you, along with all
> malice. Be kind to one another, tenderhearted,
> forgiving one another, as God in Christ forgave you.
> (Ephesians 4:31-32, ESV)

> If possible, so far as it depends on you, live peaceably
> with all. Beloved, never avenge yourselves, but leave it to
> the wrath of God, for it is written, "Vengeance is mine, I
> will repay, says the Lord." To the contrary, "if your enemy
> is hungry, feed him; if he is thirsty, give him something to
> drink; for by so doing you will heap burning coals on his
> head." (Romans 12:18-20, ESV)

Questions to Consider

1. Have you noticed toxic cycles playing out in any of your relationships (with friends, family, God, significant others, spouse)? Describe them below.

2. Is there something you feel guilt about that you can ask God's forgiveness for? Is there shame that is attacking your identity that you can let go of?

Call to Action

Write out your toxic cycle.

The toxic thought you are believing:

The way you cope with it:

Think of a person you care about. What may their toxic thoughts be? How do they cope? How do their coping mechanisms collide with yours?

Become aware of times when you've been in a cycle of shame. In what ways can you take responsibility for something you've done? What things are you taking responsibility for that God wants you to let go of?

Is God Really Good?

ADDRESSING THE MISCONCEPTIONS
THAT BLIND US TO GOD'S LOVE

STEFANIE'S STORY: GIVING UP ON GOD

I've told you how I was dumped on Valentine's Day, just three months before my wedding was to take place. It wasn't the only time my heart was left in pieces.

Let's take it back a few years to my first love in high school— Ryan. I had given him everything and trusted him with the most important parts of me, but he betrayed my trust, used and abused me, and left me feeling broken. This led me to believe the toxic thoughts that *I'm not good enough* and *I'm unlovable.* It also caused me to begin viewing all other boys as something to be used for my own benefit. I believed *Others are only objects to be used.*

The night I found out Ryan was cheating on me, he came to my house and begged for forgiveness. I didn't want to talk to him, but he had been my whole world. So late that cold, dark night I walked down the stairs and opened the porch door. He was manipulative and persuasive, twisting all the stories in his favor. He told me all our plans for a wonderful love story together were still going to come true. I was numb. Broken. Lost.

And I took him back.

But I was no longer the same girl he had been dating. My goal now was to make all of his friends like me. Getting my "degree" in flirting became my new passion—I wanted backups. I had a list of guys I would call at night, and I knew I could be in a relationship with any of them in a second. I padded my heart with as much attention as I could possibly get from them. Men were merely objects to be used for meeting my own insatiable need for validation. *Am I good enough? Pretty enough? Funny enough? Smart enough? Well-dressed enough?* I got answers to those questions from as many boys as I could. It wasn't enough.

I was still dating Ryan, but he had hardly any of my heart anymore. It had been broken apart and the pieces distributed elsewhere. Flirting became my weapon. I put on the mask of being heartless and desirable. On the outside I was a girl in a short skirt and crop top enticing as many boys as she could. But on the inside, I was hungry for attention and validation. Many young men were hurt by my careless actions toward them. It didn't faze me, though, because I believed either that men didn't have feelings or that their feelings didn't matter.

During this same time, my friend Nikki invited me to a Bible study. *A Bible study? That wouldn't be cool,* I thought. My group of friends loved to party, drink, and do drugs. But Nikki mentioned some of the people who would be there—the "cool kids"—so I agreed to go.

The atmosphere in the room was like nothing I'd ever experienced. It felt so warm and welcoming. The woman who led the study, Mrs. Steidel, was kind and shared about God's love.

I heard about Jesus in a way I never understood Him during CCD classes (my Catholic training as a child). I would talk to Mrs. Steidel afterward, telling her about the way Ryan had been treating me. She told me I was worth so much more and that I should be treated like a princess. I loved her words, and I clung to her like a second mom. A new story started to take root in my heart as I began believing what she said, but I still held my coping mechanisms close for protection. And then I got devastating news.

"I have a brain tumor, and God can heal me," Mrs. Steidel said at the next meeting. My heart sank. But the other students and I prayed that God would heal this amazing woman who was changing our lives and perspectives.

Bible study stopped for the rest of that year. My toxic thoughts quickly overtook any truth that had been trying to get a foothold. But then I got the worst news: Mrs. Steidel had died. I was crushed. Her funeral was packed with people. So many students and adults stood up and shared the impact Judy Steidel had on their lives.

After her death, I finally had the courage to break up with Ryan, and I did so in honor of Mrs. Steidel. She had changed so many lives for the better, and I wanted to be like that. My friends and I started a Bible study together my senior year. I started hanging out with the "good kids" instead of the "cool kids." I attended a ministry with them and loved what I was learning. But soon, that came crashing down too.

A rumor began circulating about the mother of one of my best friends. It turned out to be true: his mom was having an affair with the pastor of the church that hosted the ministry we were all part of. The church fell apart, its ministries ended, and the good church kids started down the same path my old friends were on—drinking, sex, and drugs.

A new toxic thought began taking root in me: *I'm the problem. I turn good people bad.*

The next year I was excited to start school at Penn State University. In spite of everything that had happened, I still wanted to make an impact on people's lives like Mrs. Steidel had. I wanted to do big things for God. I went to the extracurricular fair and paid close attention to the Christian ministry options available. I signed up for one that seemed promising and went to the first meeting.

I showed up with my mask in place—my short skirt, crop top, and lots of makeup. I said hi to the other girls, but I got cold, disinterested looks in return. They gave no indication that they wanted to be my friend. I did get a lot of attention from the boys in the group, but I went home feeling angry and rejected.

After the meeting, the accumulating pain from the last several years reached a breaking point, and I cried out in desperation:

God, if You cared about me, You wouldn't have let Ryan cheat on me. You wouldn't have let Mrs. Steidel die. You wouldn't have let the pastor have an affair with my friend's mom. You would have had the women in that group be kind to me.

God, either You are not real, or You are not good, or You could care less about me. So I'm going to care less about You too.

I promised myself that I would never be made a fool of again. I would never really give my heart to anyone else. I would always have someone or something in my back pocket—a backup plan to keep me safe. I started living a "hakuna matata" type of life—partying, boys, fun, and popularity are what I poured my heart into.

The story I convinced myself of about God became the driving force of my life. On the outside I looked happy. I looked like I was living my best life. I was dating a star football player, going to all the cool parties, going on one great vacation after another . . .

But on the inside, I was dying.

ADDRESSING OUR MISCONCEPTIONS

It's the summer of 1994, and *The Lion King* has just been released. News about it has been spreading like wildfire. As you walk into the theater, you're surprised to see the movie has already started. But you sit down quickly, because something dramatic is happening, and you're excited to see the film everyone has been talking about.

As you take your seat, you see a little lion running for his life with a stampede of wildebeests charging in fear right behind him. Then you see a scary looking lion—Scar—telling Mufasa, another huge lion, that his son Simba is in the way of the stampede, and your heart drops as the herd catches up to the cub. You feel a moment of relief as he finds a small tree to climb and get away from the trampling hooves.

Mufasa runs into the stampede, putting himself in harm's way to save his son. He places Simba on a high rock, where he will be safe, but he himself is knocked down again. Simba searches in desperation for his father, and with joy, he sees him jump up onto a rock. Mufasa claws his way up the steep cliff, and Simba runs up to try to meet his father. He doesn't see what's happening on the other side of the rock where Mufasa is calling out to Scar (his brother) for help.

As Mufasa reaches the top, Scar grasps his arms. But instead of saving his brother, he says in a sarcastic voice, "Long live the king," then throws him off the rock. From his vantage point, Simba only sees his father falling to his death.

With tears in your eyes and disappointment in your heart, you run out of the theater in shock. Everyone got it wrong. This movie is extremely upsetting.

We're guessing that if you've seen any of this movie, you've seen the whole thing. But what if the part we've just described was all you knew of the story? You entered late and exited before the end. Does that give you an accurate impression of the film?

In the same way, our lives are part of a larger story—God's story. We can look at our circumstances and label them as a hopeless disaster, but God sees redemption, hope, and so much beauty to come. We are quick to judge ourselves and the season we are in. But what if we could pull back the curtain and see the bigger picture? What if we started to tell ourselves the truth based on God's perspective?

Our lives are part of a larger story—God's story. What if we started to tell ourselves the truth based on God's perspective?

Let's go back to the movie. When we continue to watch, we see the tragic scene that comes next. Simba finds his father dead. He is devastated, and he believes the lie *I am responsible for my father's death. I have no purpose.* He runs away from his family, his home, and all of his responsibilities. He wears a mask of "hakuna matata," which means "no worries." Many people today hide behind a similar mask of "YOLO," meaning you only live once, so you might as well live it up. Don't worry about the consequences or other people. There's no greater meaning or purpose for your life, so enjoy yourself and have fun.

As the story goes on, we see that no matter how much Simba embraces the hakuna matata lifestyle, he can't escape the guilt he feels for his father's death. It's only when he's able to accept his true identity and the responsibility that he has to honor his family, his home, and his father that he learns more of the truth: He wasn't responsible for his father's death. It was his uncle who had orchestrated the whole plan. Scar had manipulated Simba and played off the lie he was believing—*My father was holding out on good things for me.* Simba's father had given him boundaries on the land—where he could roam freely and where he should not go. Scar had twisted Mufasa's words for his own purposes. But Simba finally realized the truth that his father had loved him unconditionally. He found the courage to take back what was rightfully his. The new story Simba told himself was based on truth. He was full of purpose now, and his story wasn't over. There was even redemption after the pain.

What we believe about our own story matters very much too. Are we viewing our life story through the lens of toxic cycles and pain and missing the truth? Are we seeing the full picture?

So far in our journey through this book, we've gotten really clear about defining your reasons for wanting to live wholeheartedly. Then we talked about toxic thoughts and the coping mechanisms that often follow them. We've also considered how toxic cycles might be impacting your life and the relationships you are in. With that in mind, we think this is a good time to address the misconceptions you may have about God. When we have an appropriate understanding of how He really sees us, it makes it easier to find healing from past pain or trauma, and we are better able to experience wholehearted love as God intended.

CALEB'S STORY: A VIOLATION OF TRUST

"You are definitely a shoo-in for this job."

Really?! I thought. My old English teacher felt I was a great candidate for the position I had applied for. I was surprised and humbled to hear this from someone as influential as he was in the school. If I'm being honest, though, I already thought the job was mine, since I had been coaching and substitute teaching there, and I was well on my way to earning my master's degree in education at the time.

The job was at a small Christian high school in Pasadena, California—the one I myself had attended. It was my dream teaching job to work at my old school. My parents both worked there, my mom as an art teacher (now retired), and my dad as an administrator (now the head of school). They were careful to stay out of the decision, though, because of their potential bias as well as concerns about nepotism.

After losing out on my basketball dream, I had set my sights on teaching. I had grown up around high school students, and I thought I could thrive in this familiar environment. Plus, I loved the thought of investing in the lives of students and leaving a lasting impact on them, just as my teachers had done for me. This excited me and gave me a sense of purpose again.

I had gone all in at the school, coaching most nights and taking every opportunity to serve. I chaperoned dances, went on mission trips to Central America, tutored international students—everything I could to beef up my résumé and show that I was willing to serve in any way. Let's just say, I wanted that job bad. I would have been teaching world history, my favorite subject.

So as I sat down in the large, aesthetically curated office of the head of school, I was confident I would hear the words "You're hired." But I began to sense a nervousness in the administrator. This normally warm and kind man was acting distant and professional.

His next words hit me like a bomb. "Caleb, we gave the job to someone else."

Instantaneously, his words exploded the new future I thought I was building toward. It was like a little boy setting up a battle scene with his green army soldiers. A "bomb" goes off, and he smacks the soldiers off the table. They fly in every direction, landing all around the room. That day, I felt like one of those soldiers.

I blanked out on everything else he said, almost like I was staring up at the gym ceiling again after my injury. What was God doing? I had already lost everything else. Why this?

Losing out on my new dream job was an area of great pain. I found out that people who were important to me at the school had actually been lobbying for the other person. I thought these people cared about me, and it felt like they had violated my love and trust. I felt that God had let me down as well. I had given Him this new area of my life—my old dream was dead, so I wanted to fully serve Him the only other way I knew how. But the new dream had been taken from me too.

I decided that I needed to finish my commitment at the school, but I reluctantly applied elsewhere. I eventually got a job at a rival school, leaving all that was familiar to start a new chapter in my life.

Looking back on that confusing, frustrating, and trying time, I now see the ways that God was working behind the scenes. If I had gotten that job, I would still be working there, and this book would never have been written. Millions across the globe would never have heard the gospel from me, and people who needed support from me in their relationships would not have gotten it. On top of all of that, I might never have met the woman of my dreams.

Sometimes God uses our pain for His good. The crying? Yeah, there was a ton of that. The screaming? Did that too. The questioning of whether God was good, whether He cared about me, and why I never felt good enough? God was able to redeem all of it in His timing. His perfect timing.

So how do we reconcile God's goodness with our pain when we are in the midst of it? Well, let's take a look at what Scripture says

RECONCILING GOD'S GOODNESS WITH BROKEN TRUST

When we experience violations of love and trust in our lives, it wounds us to our core and makes us tell ourselves things like *I'm not good enough* or *No one could ever love me* and maybe even *God is holding out on me.* The two of us have experienced all of these thoughts at one time or another, and it's very likely you have too.

To *violate* means to break or to disregard.[1] A violation, then, is a state of being violated, or of being broken or disregarded by someone. In a failed relationship, our hearts are broken, disregarded by the person we have entrusted everything to.

A harsh breakup leaves you feeling *not good enough* or worse, *unworthy of love*. Both are lies from the deepest, darkest pit of hell, but somehow they are a familiar tone in our heads as we deal with the aftermath of shattered dreams.

A violation of trust leads us down a road of distrust, skepticism, and cynicism. We find ourselves analyzing people and situations to make sure they are safe enough for us to approach and operate in. Broken trust is sometimes the result of being cheated on or lied to. Questions of *How long have they been lying to me?* or *Why would they go to someone else for love?* plague us when our hearts lie splintered and barren in front of us.

So how do we break free of these violations? What's the antidote?

True love's kiss.

That's it. You can close this book now. You've got the answer to everything right there.

We'd all like it to be that simple, wouldn't we? We've all had dreams of being swept away in a romance where we are the beautiful damsel in distress or the strikingly handsome knight in shining armor. One of them sweeps in to save the other with the last possible thread of hope—true love's kiss.

In the opening scene of *Once Upon a Time*, Snow White has fallen under a sleeping spell. Nothing can wake her, and hope is lost. Until Prince Charming rides valiantly across the picturesque countryside, hoping to save her from certain doom. When he kisses her, a prism of beauty rocks the world around them, and she awakes to find her prince looking at her with awe and wonder. True love has saved the day.

Something about a beautiful love story gives us hope that our own relationships won't always go the way they seem to be going, which is the wrong way. True love *is* the only thing that will save us from violations of trust, but not the love of any person. It comes only from the true Lover of Our Soul.

The truth spoken over us is like "a honeycomb, sweet to the soul and healing to the bones" (Proverbs 16:24). Kind words from our heavenly Father bring us the truth and healing we need to cover the wrongs others have done to us.

The wounds are real and are part of us, but the words of God, spoken to us and over us, are like a balm to our hearts.

Scripture tells us that true love comes only from God. Why do we have such a hard time receiving it? Why are our wounds the only voice we hear?

Scripture tells us that God is love and that true love comes only from Him (see 1 John 4:7-8). So why do we have such a hard time receiving it? Why are the wounds that have cut us so deeply the only voice we allow ourselves to hear? *Not good enough. Not worthy of love.* We've met so many people who find it easier to believe those two phrases than a book full of love letters written to them.

The problem is that we attach our worth to our experiences. There is something beautiful and innocent about the love we show others and the trust we have in them. When these are broken, we use human arguments to make sense of the pain. If God doesn't protect us from bad relationships, we believe that He can't be good. If He lets us go through difficult experiences, we believe that we aren't *worthy* of His protection or His love.

Unfortunately, that is where many people get stuck. They put on a mask over their pain, and they believe what the pain and past say about themselves and about God rather than realizing the truth.

Pulling back the curtain to see the bigger picture can change your perspective and then your life. When we see God as the main character, we understand that our pain from the violations of love and trust can all be redeemed by a God who isn't held to our timetable. His redemption, His grace, His love go beyond reason.

Our feelings matter to God. He knows we will react in certain ways when bad things happen. He doesn't want us to hide those emotions from Him. Rather, He wants us to hold on to the bigger picture because it frees us from the self-pity and self-loathing that trap us and lead only to destruction and discontent. He wants to lead us to a full and abundant life. Let's look at several aspects of God's character that are true regardless of how we feel.

God brings about good in all situations.

We know that in all things God works for the good of those who love him, who have been called according to his purpose.

ROMANS 8:28

"God is good all the time, and all the time, God is good."

This line is one of the classics of Christian culture. Watch any Christian movie, and you are bound to hear these words used to remind the main character that even in their terrible circumstances, God is still good. They are immediately encouraged and filled with hope to conquer the obstacles that they are facing.

To be honest, for the longest time, this line did nothing for us. When our hearts get broken, it's nice to hear, but how is God good even when things seem so bad?

He is good *all the time.*

Okay, Caleb and Stefanie, that's nice, but seriously though, was

God good during my abuse? Was God good when my boyfriend cheated on me? Was God good when my parents passed away?

Yes.

We are so sorry about your struggles and your loss. We hear stories from people daily that break our hearts. People go through horrible injustices, and all we have to speak from is our own experience and what God's Word says, which is that He is working for our good all the time and in every circumstance.

In order to make sense of the tough questions about God's goodness, it's vitally important to understand the rest of God's nature and who He is.

God is our Creator.

It was you who created my inward parts; you knit me together in my mother's womb.

PSALM 139:13, CSB

God designed you to be you, from the time you were in your mother's womb. And He has an amazing purpose for your life (see Jeremiah 29:11).

Did you know that when God saw the people He created, He said they were "very good"? In fact, Genesis tells us that "God saw all that he had made, and it was very good indeed" (1:31, CSB). God thinks *you* are very good. Perfectly, uniquely, and beautifully created by the ultimate Creator. Understanding this allows us to receive His love in a new way—as His creation, knowing that He delights in us as our loving Father.

The two of us have created a few things. In fact, our last book, *A Year of Prayer*, is something we are proud of. When we look at it, we delight in the fact that we worked to write and be involved in every part of putting together that book. In the same way, God delights in the design, the work, and the creativity that He put into you. You are very good to Him, and the way He felt about you the day you were born hasn't changed.

God never changes.

> Do you not know? Have you not heard? The Lord is the everlasting God, the Creator of the whole earth. He never becomes faint or weary; there is no limit to his understanding. He gives strength to the faint and strengthens the powerless.
>
> ISAIAH 40:28-29, CSB

God never changes. He doesn't get tired, He never grows faint or weary. We don't know about you, but the most tiring thing imaginable to us would be running a marathon. Running 26.2 miles sounds like the worst thing a person could do. But running a marathon would be a piece of cake for God. Backward, forward, it wouldn't matter. He never changes.

The book of Hebrews tells us that "Jesus Christ is the same yesterday, today, and forever" (13:8, CSB). Jesus in His very nature is God (see Philippians 2:6), a part of the Trinity along with the Father and the Holy Spirit. If Jesus never changes, that means that God is the same yesterday, today, tomorrow—the day you were hurt, today in your mess, and the day you will get better. He is always the same. So if He is good in the times you experience joy, He is just as good when you are experiencing your worst pain. God's goodness is not dictated by circumstance or timing. He is good, period.

God is love.

> We have come to know and to believe the love that God has for us. God is love, and the one who remains in love remains in God, and God remains in him.
>
> 1 JOHN 4:16, CSB

God is the embodiment of love. We see this in His actions throughout the Bible and in the lives of those who love Him. How does the Bible characterize love?

> Love is patient, love is kind. Love does not envy, is not boastful, is not arrogant, is not rude, is not self-seeking, is not irritable, and does not keep a record of wrongs. Love finds no joy in unrighteousness but rejoices in the truth. It bears all things, believes all things, hopes all things, endures all things. Love never ends.
>
> 1 CORINTHIANS 13:4-8, CSB

As a culture, we like thinking of love in this way. These verses are the sermon topic at many weddings each year, whether Christian or secular. But if we believe that 1 John is true, we can substitute God's name for love throughout these verses. If God is love, then God is patient, God is kind . . . God never ends.

There it is again. God is always the same, He never ends. And if He is love, then His love never ends. Receive that today—that God is love, and His love for you has never ended. It continues today, tomorrow, and every day into the future. He will always be loving you, His "very good" creation. And He will love you each day, whether it's your worst or your best.

God is present.

> Be strong and courageous. Do not be afraid or terrified because of them, for the LORD your God goes with you; he will never leave you nor forsake you.
>
> DEUTERONOMY 31:6

When you were going through the worst pain, God was with you. When you felt the most alone you've ever felt, God was with you. Even when you tried to push Him away, He was with you. He won't abandon you.

God is our ever-present helper and counselor (see Psalm 46:1). One of the things we love most about Him is that He sits with us in our pain. Think of Joseph being thrown in prison when he had done nothing wrong. God was with him, comforting him. And when the time was right, He elevated him to a high position of leadership in Egypt. Joseph could have cursed God in those difficult years, but he stayed faithful, and his righteousness was seen and blessed by God.

In the same way, God is there with you, and He wants to be near you. It is His nature to be with us at all times, even when it feels like He's not.

God is peace.

Peace I leave with you. My peace I give to you. I do not give to you as the world gives. Don't let your heart be troubled or fearful.

JOHN 14:27, CSB

God is peace. In Him we can find rest for our souls. Life is filled with worry. Worry about having enough food, making enough money, finding the love of our lives. But in God, we can find the peace we need to cover all of our worries.

We tend to equate our worries with God's character. We think that since our worries have not gone away and our troubles still haunt us, that must mean that God isn't good. The mistake here is that we believe God's goodness is tied to our worries and troubles. It's hard for our human minds to comprehend, but the apostle Paul tells us that "the peace of God, which surpasses all understanding, will guard your hearts and minds in Christ Jesus" (Philippians 4:7, CSB). In ways we don't entirely understand,

God's peace covers our troubles when we are able to lay them at His feet. His character is peaceful.

How do we receive God's peace when we are still in the midst of our pain?

By growing closer to Him. Spending time with Him. Delighting in His presence. Look at this verse and you'll see what we mean: "Be gracious to me, God, be gracious to me, for I take refuge in you. I will seek refuge in the shadow of your wings until danger passes" (Psalm 57:1, csb).

Notice that it mentions taking shelter under His wings. You'd have to be pretty close to a bird to be under its wings. In the same way, we have to grow close to our heavenly Father to experience the peace and protection that comes from being in His presence. Here is the result when we do: "Finally, brothers and sisters, rejoice. Become mature, be encouraged, be of the same mind, be at peace, and the God of love and peace will be with you" (2 Corinthians 13:11, csb). Oftentimes we don't know His peace because we aren't seeking His presence daily. We enjoy His peace as we grow closer to Him.

God is grace.

All have sinned and fall short of the glory of God.

ROMANS 3:23, CSB

We all fall short of God's glory. The wrongs we do, the sins we commit, all of it means we are deserving of death. As it says in Romans 6, "the wages of sin is death, but the gift of God is eternal life in Christ Jesus our Lord" (verse 23, csb). We deserve to be punished, but it is by the great love and grace of God that we get to experience abundant life here on earth and eternal life afterward. He separates our sins from us as far as the east is from the west (see Psalm 103:12).

Too often, we think because God isn't taking care of the pain in our lives that He doesn't love us. That He has forgotten about us. This toxic thought can ring in our heads: *God must be holding out on me.*

The truth to replace that thought with is this: *God loves me and He cares about me.* In fact, this is how much He cares for you: "God loved the world in this way: He gave his one and only Son, so that everyone who believes in him will not perish but have eternal life" (John 3:16, CSB).

There is nothing you can do to deserve this, there's nothing you can do to earn it. It's a gift of God's grace to you, covering all of your sins and bringing you into the fullness of His love. God is good all the time because all the time He has forgiven you of every sin you have committed and every sin you will ever commit. He is just *that good.*

God is good.

> Give thanks to the LORD, for he is good; his faithful love endures forever.
>
> 1 CHRONICLES 16:34, CSB

God's goodness is not dictated by circumstances, by feelings, by wrongful actions, nor any type of human wisdom. God's goodness is dictated by who He is. And He is love, He is grace, He is unchanging, He is Creator, He is peace, and so much more.

Friend, your pain is real. You may still have many questions about it. *Why did it happen to me while someone else was protected from it?* There are no simple answers. But what is true is that God is good no matter what happens. It's His nature, it's the way He has been throughout time, and it's the way He will continue to be.

What God truly wants is a relationship with you, to be close to you. He wants you to draw near to Him, and He will draw near to you (see James 4:8). The last thing God wants is for you to be uncertain about His goodness. He wants abundant life for you, friend. And abundant life comes from knowing God and walking in close relationship with Him. That's when the truths of these Scriptures come alive. We experience God the best when we are with Him the most. He has never left you, and He never will (see Deuteronomy 31:6).

God is good all the time, and all the time, God is good.

God chose us.

He chose us in him before the creation of the world to be holy and blameless in his sight. In love he predestined us for adoption to sonship through Jesus Christ, in accordance with his pleasure and will—to the praise of his glorious grace, which he has freely given us in the One he loves. In him we have redemption through his blood, the forgiveness of sins, in accordance with the riches of God's grace that he lavished on us.

EPHESIANS 1:4-8

Did you catch that? God *chose* you before the creation of the world. It may feel more like truth to believe you were *not* chosen. All the past rejection from friends, family, school, work, and so on can make that feel like the truth, but it's not. You were chosen by the one who created the world.

And the good news doesn't end there. When we accept Jesus, God no longer sees us for our old identity. He sees us as new creations, holy and without blame. As Paul tells us, "If anyone is in Christ, the new creation has come: The old has gone, the new is here!" (2 Corinthians 5:17). A chapter later, we learn that God has adopted us into His family: "I will be a Father to you, and you will be my sons and daughters, says the Lord Almighty" (2 Corinthians 6:18).

We are children of God when we receive Jesus. We are daughters and sons of the King of kings. And He loves us beyond measure.

Going back to *The Lion King*, you might say, "I'm not like Simba. He was the son of a king." According to Scripture, his story might hit closer to home than you think.

And you may resonate with parts of Emma's story in *Once Upon a Time*. She thought she was an orphan, but the truth is that she was born out of true love. She felt like no one cared about her, but she had people who loved her more than she could have imagined. You might be thinking, *Stef and Caleb, that is only a fairy tale. She may have been made from true love, but not me.*

Maybe you were the result of a one-night stand. Maybe you don't know your birth parents. Maybe you've felt like you were a "mistake." Any of these might be part of your story, but they're not the truest part. There is something that trumps every single one of these things: the fact that the God of the universe chose you before the creation of the world. He calls you by name and you are His.

No matter how you came into this world, no matter what has happened to you, no matter what toxic thoughts you believe about yourself, you have a truer identity that God wants you to know about. He wants you as His beloved child, and He is the perfect Father. You are not a mistake to God. You are His masterpiece. He wants to reframe the way you are treated, and He wants to lavish His perfect love on you.

> *God wants to reframe the way you are treated, and He wants to lavish His perfect love on you.*

In *The Lion King*, Nala and Rafiki sought out Simba to help him find his true identity. Simba was resistant. It was easier to believe the toxic thoughts. In *Once Upon a Time*, Emma's son sought her out and did everything he could to lead her to her true identity. But her eyes were blinded by her experiences and trauma. It was much easier to believe the toxic thoughts.

Finally, Simba's eyes were opened when he heard his father's voice. Emma's eyes were opened when her son sacrificed his life for hers in a heroic act.

In the same way, Jesus sacrificed everything for us, so we can know our true identity in Him. He paid the ultimate price so we wouldn't have to. He carried our sin, our pain, and our shame with Him to the cross, so that we can walk in His truth.

He came to show us the larger story. Are you ready to embrace your story through a brand-new lens?

We have taken you on quite a journey so far. We described toxic thoughts and how they cause us to cope in ways that trap us in cycles of pain (even in our relationships with others). But gratefully, God is good, and His goodness doesn't change despite the circumstances we find ourselves in. Understanding the goodness of God is paramount for moving forward because as you will soon find out, we often must reach the end of our rope before we are ready to make a change.

MAKING IT PERSONAL

Scripture to Apply

We invite you to read the following verses and note how God describes the truth, as well as what new beginnings mean for us as we choose to follow Him in our lives. You can summarize what you see in these verses in the space provided below.

> Gracious words are a honeycomb, sweet to the soul and healing to the bones. (Proverbs 16:24)

He chose us in him before the creation of the world to be holy and blameless in his sight. In love he predestined us for adoption to sonship through Jesus Christ, in accordance with his pleasure and will—to the praise of his glorious grace, which he has freely given us in the One he loves. In him we have redemption through his blood, the forgiveness of sins, in accordance with the riches of God's grace that he lavished on us. (Ephesians 1:4-8)

I will be a Father to you, and you will be my sons and daughters, says the Lord Almighty. (2 Corinthians 6:18)

Therefore, if anyone is in Christ, the new creation has come: The old has gone, the new is here! (2 Corinthians 5:17)

Peace I leave with you. My peace I give to you. I do not give to you as the world gives. Don't let your heart be troubled or fearful. (John 14:27, csb)

Here are a few additional verses you may wish to look up if you have time: 1 Chronicles 16:34; John 3:16; 1 Timothy 4:4; 1 John 4:8, 16.

Questions to Consider

1. What things have you been blaming God for in your life?

2. How can you choose to see His goodness all around you, even in painful times?

Call to Action

The best way to see God's goodness and appreciate His blessings is to practice gratitude. Grab a pen and paper, or use the notes app on your phone, and write down ten things you are thankful for right now. Big or small, it doesn't matter. Just be as specific as you can. Then do this every day. You will begin to be more aware of all the good things God has done in your life, and it will change your perspective on your situation.

At the End of Your Rope

SURRENDERING TO GOD
WHEN THE PAIN BECOMES UNBEARABLE

STEFANIE'S STORY: ROBOT MODE

My hair was slicked back and wet after my nightly shower. I was cozy in my pink heart bed shorts and pink T-shirt. I pulled out my two books. One of them I'd been writing in almost every night for a year, recording a brief description of what I had done that day. The other was a fresh, new, blue-flowered journal.

I'd just finished another like it filled with the preceding two months of writing to my twin baby boys. I'd written a poem to them every night since I found out they had died inside of me. Routine was what had been getting me through the last several months of pain. But our usual schedule—the only thing holding me together—had been disrupted recently.

On this night, the emotions I'd been hiding from myself for months, maybe even years, started to well up inside of me. I burst into one of those intense, sobbing ugly cries. Caleb reacted immediately. Sitting down next to me on the bed, he scooted close and held me tight. I rested my head on him, and tears started streaming onto his shoulder.

"What's going on?" he asked me gently. "Why are you so sad?" He's accustomed to my occasional emotional spells. But this one was different.

"I want to shut off my heart for good. It hurts too much," I said through sobs. As I reflected, I realized I'd been shutting down for a while now. Putting up walls instead of fences to certain people. Going on autopilot.

"I've been going into 'robot bitter shrew mode,'" I said. It was a revelation. It wasn't something I'm proud of, but it helped me survive the trauma of losing my long-prayed-for babies.

And it felt so hypocritical. *I'm in the midst of writing a book about wholehearted love, and I've been slowly shutting off love from my life.*

This new realization placed a crossroads in front of me.

I understand that putting on a mask was important for me during that time, and that it still can be important for getting from one day to the next. Sometimes we have to hide for a season. Sometimes we need to find the healthiest way we can to cope with trauma and pain.

But I don't want that to be my whole story. I was shutting off loving and being loved. I was shutting off seeing and being seen. I was shutting off being known and getting to know others.

I wanted to email our editor right then and there. I wanted to say, "I'm quitting this book. It's too hard. I'm ready to quit trying for more children. It's too scary. I want to stop loving others so much. It's too painful. I will be a shadow of who I was. That will be safe."

With tears still streaming, I told Caleb, "When my babies were inside of me there were three of us. With both of them dying it feels like two-thirds of me has gone away. And it's not the best version of me that remains."

Caleb let me cry as he asked questions for over an hour. He was grieving as well. I had seen the tears flow down his face the day we found out the sad news. He was grieving in his own way and also constantly trying to check in on me. He was so sweet and comforting, but he also reminded me of our wedding vows. "We told each other 'I will love you in the good times and the bad,'" he said. "Did you mean that, Stefanie?"

I put myself in his shoes. I wanted him to love me wholeheartedly. I wanted that more than almost anything in the world. How was it fair that I wanted that so badly from him but was slowly shutting off my heart? Not only would I not be able to receive love from him, but I wouldn't be able to give it either.

THE BATTLE WITHIN

When we are bombarded with sorrows, lies, failures, and defeats, another battle rages *within* us. It's the battle between truth and toxic thoughts. And when we've come close to the end of our rope, it becomes easier and easier to believe what appears to be happening right in front of us. It's easier and easier for truth to be overpowered by our feelings. That's why continually claiming the truth as you process and pour out your heart before God is vital in these moments. As you continue reading, remember this: your pain is not the end of the story.

So far, we have shown you how to identify toxic thoughts and the actions—coping—that happen because of them. You've learned how to see the unhealthy cycles in your life and how they keep you spinning in circles. And we dived deep into the goodness of God in the last chapter, seeing that He is still there with you even in the midst of your pain.

But what about those times you've given your all, but because of the downpour of pain, confusion, frustration, and loss after loss, you're on the verge of quitting? That's exactly how we felt this year, even as we were writing this to you.

Over the last several months since we lost our babies, Stefanie had been fighting the lie *I'm a failure*. This is what *shame* says. It was a toxic thought about herself, and—if you have ever battled this feeling—it is a huge lie about you too. God made you and He doesn't make failures. He knit you together in your mother's womb. You are chosen, loved, and cherished. That is your identity. No matter what life brings your way, you are *never* a failure. We assure you, you can find healing from your past pain or trauma, and you can experience wholehearted love as God intended.

THE BLAME GAME

When something very difficult happens, many of us look for someone to blame. After the loss of the twins, I (Stefanie) found myself at first asking, *Did I fail? Did God fail?* As I've wrestled with these questions, I've realized that neither of us did.

What I choose to believe right now is extremely important, and it's going to have a big impact on the rest of my life. I've had to forgive God for the anger I held against Him. I've had to forgive myself for the anger I've held against me. But I didn't fail. I need to choose the truth even when my feelings are saying something different. There's nothing I could have done to prevent the loss of my babies. By recognizing this, I have the choice of moving forward in the truth and in healing.

As I write this, I have so many friends who are pregnant, with their sweet babies due right around the same time as Shiloh and Asher would have been. As I see their baby bumps growing, see them honored with baby showers, see them celebrate as I mourn, it's hard not to feel like the world is moving on without me and I'm stuck.

If you feel this way about any area of your life, I hope and pray you will run to Jesus' arms and to God's Word. If you feel stuck, if your heart feels broken, if you sense others moving on while you're running in place, God has redemption waiting for you, even if you can't see it yet.

He is ministering to me. He is reminding me of my worth. He is teaching me to forgive myself, to be kind in

God has redemption waiting for you, even if you can't see it yet.

how I think about my body, and to believe the truth that even though I may face hardship and trouble in this world, He has overcome the world (see John 16:33). His plans for me are still good. He hasn't forgotten about me.

Please remind yourself that God has not forgotten you either. You are *not* a failure despite any mistakes you may have made. We like to point to someone's mistakes or sin as a reason for their suffering. But God's Word says something very different. When asked about the reason for a man's blindness, Jesus said, "Neither this man nor his parents sinned . . . but this happened so that the works of God might be displayed in him" (John 9:3). In other words, the man's blindness was not due to any wrongdoing on his part, but rather it was an opportunity for him to experience God at work in his life.

Trouble can come to any of us, but even through the worst times, God is good. He holds us close and teaches us more about His love. Jesus hates the pain we face, so much so that He came to this earth to bring life and healing. And He died to conquer death once and for all.

Often, when we believe the lie *I am a failure*, it's because we made a mistake. We've all made mistakes. We all have sinned and fallen short. But God has made us each a masterpiece. We are not the sum of our mistakes. We are new creations in Christ. When we've done something wrong, we can ask God for forgiveness, and He removes our sins as far as the east is from the west.

Knowing this, we can switch our thinking so it is not identity based—so that our mistakes are not about who we *are*, but rather about what we have *done*. We can reflect on our mistakes, and we can pray that God will grow us to do better in the future.

In this difficult time, I (Stefanie) made the decision to love Jesus and Caleb wholeheartedly even though it's painful. We prayed together, vowing not to bring up past sins and mistakes, but to move forward in wholehearted love with each other and God.

I slept in peace that night, feeling closer to God and Caleb than I had in such a long time. Caleb met me in my vulnerability. He fought for my heart. He expressed his desire for my *full* heart. He reminded me that I don't have to get over my babies' death immediately—I probably never will be completely over it. But allowing him and Jesus to enter into my pain, and being real and vulnerable with them, is worth it.

THE COST OF WHOLEHEARTED LOVE

Have you hit this crossroads in your life? Trauma or disappointment has struck, and the pain seems too much. You've put on your mask, and you wonder if you should close off your heart forever. Pouring your energies into material things, hobbies, sports, fashion, entertainment, or Hollywood gossip seems easier, safer. But it will cost you so much, as C. S. Lewis explains:

> To love at all is to be vulnerable. Love anything, and your heart will certainly be wrung and possibly be broken.
> If you want to make sure of keeping it intact, you must

give your heart to no one, not even to an animal. Wrap it carefully round with hobbies and little luxuries; avoid all entanglements; lock it up safe in the casket or coffin of your selfishness. But in that casket—safe, dark, motionless, airless—it will change. It will not be broken; it will become unbreakable, impenetrable, irredeemable.[1]

I (Stefanie) got to this point. *Let me pour myself into other things*, I thought. *Let me just become a shell of who I was.* But no. Thankfully, I tasted the beauty of being fully seen, known, and loved by God and by Caleb. And I don't want to go back. Even though it might sometimes feel safer.

As I sit here writing these words, tears are streaming down my face again. My heart is still shattered in pieces because of my babies. And I think of you reading this and the pain you may have traveled through. I wish I could invite you over for tea today. As we sat on my cozy couch overlooking the forest, we could have a deep talk about the hurt in your life that has made you put on your masks. The pain that makes you wish you could remove your heart from your chest.

Even though you and I can't be together in person, God is here to sit with you today. He's ready to listen. You can pour your heart out fully to Him. He's not afraid of your tears. He collects them in a bottle (see Psalm 56:8). I know He has an extra-big bottle for me. How big is His bottle for you?

STEFANIE'S STORY: GOING ALL IN

As I think about this pivotal moment in my life now, my thoughts rewind to a time sixteen years ago. Do you remember my story from the last chapter? When I decided that God didn't care about me, so I turned away from Him?

I spent two years on that path of partying and "hakuna matata." Although I looked so happy, fun, and full of life, inside I was dying. There was so much pain in my past that I was trying to hide from others. I covered it up with the parties, boys, trying hard in school, and working to get the "good life." But the pain was surfacing anyway. The drinking caused depression, and suicidal thoughts became something I battled every day.

I told one of my friends my desire to end my life, and how I didn't see a point anymore. He told me, "Why don't you try going all in with God? You've been one foot in and one foot out for all your life. What do you have to lose by giving Him *everything?*"

It was true. I grew up Catholic and always had a love for God. I loved Jesus and went to church every Saturday with my family. But during the week, I lied to my dad to sneak out to parties and stay at Ryan's house. I claimed to have a love for God but really did whatever I thought was cool and made me important. I had thrown off trying to live for God and had dived fully into the "good life" . . . which wasn't turning out all that good after all.

My friend gave me some Christian songs and sermons to listen to. I was intrigued by them and longed for something more. At the beginning of my junior year, I signed up for a Christian ministry to help high school students learn about Jesus.

At the meeting, they described what they expected from us as leaders. *Whoa!* I thought. *I'm going to have to change everything about my life if I do this!*

Afterward, I sat at the computer desk in my apartment, staring at the screen. *Should I go all in with God? Even if that means everything is about to change?* I decided, *Yes.*

I told God, *I'm all in, all of me, my whole heart. You can have it all.* I was at the end of my rope and at the beginning of a whole new adventure of being loved to the depths of my pain like I'd never experienced before. Jesus' love became more real than any-thing else in the months to come. I was amazed at how His love was healing dark places of my soul I had hidden away for years.

Now fast-forward to the moment I wanted to close off my heart. I thought back to this time at the desk in my apartment. I remember God's love being big enough to hold all my pain, shame, mistakes, questions, and longings then. If it was true then, why couldn't it be true now?

I'm going all in, Jesus, I prayed once again. *I give You all my heart, all my pain, all that's left of me. I trust You to build back my life and heart again. I want to tell myself Your version of my story.*

HEARTS ON HOLIDAY

Have you seen the movie *The Holiday*? One of the main characters, Amanda, finds out at the beginning that her boyfriend has been cheating on her. She tries to cry but can't shed a tear. It turns out that she hasn't been able to cry for a very long time.

She decides to book a vacation, leaving her Los Angeles home to travel to England over Christmas. Instead of feeling less alone in the charming cottage, she finds herself feeling more alone than ever—until she meets a man named Graham and they connect in a way she hadn't with anyone else. She opens up about the fact that she hasn't cried since her parents told her they were getting divorced and she saw her dad's packed suitcase on the floor. She and her parents had always been "the three musketeers," and she never recovered from the trio being broken apart.

When Amanda visits Graham's house, she finds out that he has two children and is a widower. They share a darling time, the four of them, and the girls adore Amanda. One of the daughters tells Amanda they call themselves "the three musketeers." The words are redeeming for Amanda and at the same time seem like fate.

As their romance continues, Graham confesses that he is in love with Amanda. But they know she will soon return to Los Angeles. They say their goodbyes and Amanda is in the town car, headed back to the airport. As she's driving away and reflecting on her holiday, tears start to flow. She's shocked and amazed! She starts laughing and tells the driver to turn around. Her heart, shut down for so many years, has finally opened again. The narrator says, "Amanda Woods, welcome back!" She returns to the house to find Graham sobbing over her departure, and she lets him know she will stay longer.

After the vulnerability of opening up to Caleb and making the brave decision to stop shutting down my heart to him and God, it was as if I (Stefanie) heard a narrator over my own life saying, "Stefanie Rouse, welcome back!"

If you are at a similar breaking point, you might be asking, "What if it hurts again? What if I get burned?"

But what if it's beautiful? What if it's wonderful? What if you open up your heart to God, being fully encompassed by His love, and it's better than you ever imagined? What if there are beautiful new parts of your heart that are yet to be opened? What if the closing off was causing you more harm and pain than you've realized? What if giving over that control into His loving arms sets you free?

Amanda Woods was back when she allowed her heart to be open to love again. For her, the toxic thoughts of:

Everyone will leave.
Everything good will end, so I might as well not love anything.

. . . were met with another reality:

What if they don't leave?
What if good can last?

What if closing my heart and pushing others away isn't my best option?

For me, the toxic thoughts of:

I'm a mistake.
Everyone close to me will get hurt, so I must shut out everyone.

. . . turned into:

God can make a message even out of my mess.
God is healing me and wants me to be a part of helping others heal.

Dear one, what lies have been at the forefront of many of your decisions? Is fear determining your life and your path? Is it time to let God lead instead?

THE DECISION IS YOURS

Many people in the Bible dealt with the pain and shame of past mistakes and trauma. Each of them faced the same decision we do: *Will we allow Jesus into the pain? Will we love with our whole heart?* Consider the woman who encountered Jesus as He walked among a big crowd of people who were following Him:

> Just then a woman who had been subject to bleeding for twelve years came up behind him and touched the edge of his cloak. She said to herself, "If I only touch his cloak, I will be healed."
>
> Jesus turned and saw her. "Take heart, daughter," he said, "your faith has healed you." And the woman was healed at that moment.
>
> MATTHEW 9:20-22

Twelve years of intense suffering, and Jesus healed her in an instant. Not only that, but Jesus called her "daughter." She was probably suffering from relational wounds in addition to her physical disorder. Back then, when you had a medical issue such as this, you were cast aside and often considered "unclean." Can you imagine if your family viewed you this way? But Jesus gave her a place to belong. She was no longer "the sick girl who is always bleeding." She was "daughter."

God is the same yesterday, today, and forever. He is the same God today as when He healed that woman. She didn't give up through the suffering. She had likely sought out many doctors, and she finally found her Healer.

When we are met fully by Jesus in His presence, when we surrender to Him and experience His life-giving love, it's hard not to overflow with praise. As the lyrics to "Whole Heart" that I (Stefanie) sing so often declare:

So here I stand
High in surrender
I need You now

Hold my heart
Now and forever
My soul cries out

Once I was broken
But You loved my whole heart through
Sin has no hold on me
'Cause Your grace holds me now.[2]

The word *surrender* is defined as "to abandon oneself entirely to (a powerful emotion or influence); give in to."[3] In my act of surrender to Jesus and Caleb I got my heart back. I surrendered my pain, shame, and fear to Jesus. I gave God my burdens. And as I keep handing them over as situations change, I get peace in exchange for fear. I get love instead of hate. I become sweet instead of bitter. Instead of being robotic, I am present, loving, and real.

My prayers changed everything for me.

Have plans and hopes fallen through recently in your own life? Are you feeling disappointed or discouraged? Or perhaps the state of the world in general has you ready to give up. We promise, friend, that what the enemy has taken years to destroy, Jesus can redeem in a day.

Where in your life do you need to reach out to Jesus for redemption and healing?

No matter how distant you feel from

No matter how distant you feel from Him, He isn't far. Will you be bold enough to reach out for Him?

Him, He isn't far. He's not scared of your past. You don't have to be clean to come to Him. He loves you right in your mess, right in your disappointment. Will you be bold enough to reach out for Him like the woman in the crowd?

We encourage you to call to God. Open up the Bible. Let the Holy Spirit speak to your soul. Let God call you by your real name—daughter or son. Let Jesus give you a place of belonging, redemption, hope, identity, and healing. As Jesus told the woman, He wants you also to "go in peace and be freed from your suffering" (Mark 5:34). You have purpose, and your story isn't over. He doesn't always heal us in an instant, but sometimes He does. And He always comes through. He's there for you today.

PUTTING PAIN IN ITS PLACE

It is normal to feel pain and to experience the emotions that go along with it. But when we experience pain in our hearts, it impacts how we go about our lives. The thing is, if you don't put pain in its rightful place, eventually it's going to spill over into everything else around it.

Pain is kind of like fire. When left unchecked, a fire can ravage a countryside and burn things that weren't meant to be touched by it. Pain works the same way. It needs to be kept in check. Coping with your pain may serve you for a time. But, eventually, like anyone else, you will come to a breaking point.

Think about learning to ride a bicycle. At first, it's really hard. The bike usually has a set of training wheels on the back for support. They serve a purpose for a season, to protect the rider. Eventually, the child is able to get along without them, and it's time to take the training wheels off. You see the excitement as the child builds up speed and the streamers blow fiercely in the wind. There might be some bumps and bruises along the way without those wheels, but the freedom of going faster, taking turns harder, and fully experiencing all that the bike has to offer is worth the transition.

Similarly, our masks and coping mechanisms help protect us for a time. But, like training wheels, they can also teach us bad habits if we hang on to them for too long. When we first "take the wheels off" we have a hard time staying up on our own. So we go back—back to the pain, back to the behaviors that helped us in the difficult season. This is why so many people get stuck.

The problem builds, and we find ourselves at a breaking point. We need to deal with our pain, and the only way to do that is to place it before the feet of Jesus. Only He can contain it. Only He can soothe the wounds from a broken heart or the abuse of a family member. Only Jesus can wash away the guilt and shame of the past and make it brand new. He alone can truly fill the hole in your heart. As Jesus says in the book of Revelation, "I am making everything new!" (21:5).

Jesus wants to take away the pain you have experienced. He

wants to take the burden you have been carrying, the pain of being rejected, the hurt of feeling unwanted, the agony of broken trust— all of those feelings that sit on our shoulders like huge boulders if we allow them to. They weigh us down, making it difficult to see what's ahead. But Jesus says in Matthew 11:28-29, "Come to me, all you who are weary and burdened, and I will give you rest. Take my yoke upon you and learn from me, for I am gentle and humble in heart, and you will find rest for your souls."

Jesus desires for us to come to Him for rest. Only in Him will we find it.

You have a choice: Are you going to let pain rule you, or are you going to put it in its rightful place?

"But wait! John took my virginity and then left me for another girl the next day!" Jesus can take that from you. He sees you, daughter. He loves you.

"But Jessica told me she loved me, then ran off with another man." Jesus still loves you and will never leave you.

"But my father screamed at me and hit me when he was drunk!" God is your loving Father, He created you in your mother's womb, and all He wants is for you to run to His loving arms.

You see, coping with our pain is a remedy. But it doesn't cure what is only curable through Jesus. Your pain is real. It's palpable. You experience it whenever you go out and see another couple walking together. It takes you right back to your moment of pain. That's okay, you are allowed to feel that pain. But you have a choice: Are you going to let that pain rule you, or are you going to put it in its rightful place?

THE IMPOSSIBLE BECOMES POSSIBLE

Audrey Hepburn said, "Nothing is impossible. The word itself says, 'I'm Possible'!" The message is that you can do anything, and no one can stop you. While that's true in a sense, it focuses on what we can achieve. The two of us have achieved a lot in our lives, but we couldn't overcome the pain from our pasts on our own. So while yes, we might be able to do "anything," we believe a better perspective on the impossible is what Jesus said: "With man this is impossible, but with God all things are possible" (Matthew 19:26).

Overcoming our pain, hurt, and abuse on our own is impossible. But when we submit it to God, it becomes possible.

This doesn't mean that once we give it to God, everything is perfect. We still struggle, we still have pain, but we don't have to carry it anymore. We aren't meant to carry burdens; God wants to carry them for us. We weren't meant to have to deal with the sin and heartache in our world. We weren't created for that. We were created to live wholeheartedly with God, enjoying the fullness of life.

So we encourage you today to take your emotional burden and place it on Jesus' shoulders. He can carry it. When He was beaten almost to the point of death, He carried a cross almost half a mile. He can surely bear any load you bring to Him.

Take in the truth about who God is—that He is for you, not against you. That He never left you even in your worst moments. Let this truth be your anchor as we tackle how to replace those toxic thoughts you are believing about yourself, others, and God. Let's find out together how to replace them with the truth. We will uncover how you can do this in the heat of the moment, even if everything around you is telling you otherwise. There is hope and purpose for your pain.

Please take some time to read these Scriptures below. Note how God is a refuge for you in the midst of your pain and how He stays near you no matter what you are facing. Summarize what you see in these verses in the space provided below.

Scripture to Apply

You keep track of all my sorrows. You have collected all my tears in your bottle. You have recorded each one in your book. (Psalm 56:8, NLT)

"He will wipe every tear from their eyes. There will be no more death" or mourning or crying or pain, for the old order of things has passed away. (Revelation 21:4)

Even though I walk through the valley of the shadow of death, I will fear no evil, for you are with me; your rod and your staff, they comfort me. (Psalm 23:4, ESV)

The LORD himself goes before you and will be with you; he will never leave you nor forsake you. Do not be afraid; do not be discouraged. (Deuteronomy 31:8)

I have told you these things, so that in me you may have peace. In this world you will have trouble. But take heart! I have overcome the world. (John 16:33)

The LORD is close to the brokenhearted and saves those who are crushed in spirit. (Psalm 34:18)

Here are a few additional verses you may wish to look up if you have time: Psalm 126:5; Lamentations 3:20-24; Matthew 5:4; 1 Peter 5:7.

Questions to Consider

1. In what ways have you been hiding from God, yourself, or others?

2. Has part of you felt closed off? Describe how that plays out in your life.

3. Are you ready to have God heal and redeem your pain? What feelings do you have as you consider being free from your past burdens?

Call to Action

Pray this prayer over your life:

Dear Jesus, thank You that You enter into my pain, shame, and guilt. As I surrender all of this to Your loving hands, I know You have something wonderful to give me in exchange. You have a life of love, goodness, and grace for me. Thank You for always being near me. I invite You into my heart and into every aspect of my life today. Will You walk beside me? I need Your help. Will You please help me to release these burdens into Your hands? You're so faithful to take my cares and worries. Please exchange my anxiety for peace, my pain for joy, and my hurt for forgiveness and love. Thanks for Your amazing love for me. I need You, Jesus. Amen.

7

The Truth Sets Us Free

REPLACING HURTFUL THOUGHTS
WITH TRUTHS FROM GOD'S WORD

CALEB'S STORY: INCOMPLETE PASS

You could feel the weight of the game like a sack of cement on each shoulder. I sensed the tension even through the television, as if I were sitting there on the sideline with the team. Green Bay, Wisconsin, in January, freezing temperatures and football . . . this was going to be a game to remember. But not in the way I thought.

It was fourth down, and the Cowboys (my favorite football team) were down by five points in the fourth quarter, with five minutes left in the game, in the divisional round of the playoffs. The two teams had been locked in a tight matchup all afternoon, and the winner looked the sure favorite to play in the Super Bowl that year. Huge plays by each team made this game seem like it was going to be an instant classic.

Tony Romo, the Cowboys quarterback, got the ball and threw

a pass downfield to Dez Bryant (wide receiver, and my favorite player at the time) who made an unbelievable acrobatic catch. After jumping over the defender to catch the ball, he landed on both feet and in the same motion dived for the end zone. The immediate call was touchdown, and it looked like the Cowboys were in the driver's seat to win the game. I went crazy, cheering loudly and jumping around with joy over the incredible play.

Moments later, the unthinkable happened. During an NFL game, the officials review scoring plays to see if the player did anything that would discount the point. And in this review, they deemed the pass incomplete.

I went ballistic! I was screaming and yelling profanities about everyone involved in a way I am not proud of and hope I will never repeat.

I felt completely cheated out of an outcome to a season I thought was "the one." My own worth was so tied to the fate of my favorite team that I felt defeated and frustrated. In my rage, I lost any concept of reality and threw a massive temper tantrum like a little boy whose favorite toy has been taken away.

Once I stopped yelling, I saw my cute, new wife huddled over in the corner of the couch, shaking and scared. This was in our first year of marriage, and Stefanie was probably wondering at that moment who this person was. Seeing her trembling was like daggers to my soul. I was deeply crushed to see her reaction.

Because of the loss of my own sports career, there was a hole in me that wanted to be filled with success and victory. My toxic thoughts of *I'm a failure* and *I'm not good enough* still were deep inside my soul. To compensate, I had attached much of my worth—without my truly realizing it—to the Dallas Cowboys and my other favorite teams, causing me to overreact in a way that was outside of my character. If they won, I was *good enough*. If they didn't, I was *a failure*.

After the game, I felt immense shame, like I was a horrible person who didn't deserve love. My wife, feeling triggered by my behavior, which brought up emotions from the abuse in her past, began to cry. I had sworn to protect her, provide for her, and make her feel safe. And I can promise you, those were the last things she was feeling in that moment.

My immediate response was to justify my behavior by placing blame on the refs. To be honest, I didn't want to face the shame I felt. But how could I defend myself? I spent some time calming down and then took full responsibility for my actions. Calmly, carefully, respectfully.

I will never forget how Stefanie responded to me. She did say that I had to earn the right to have her watch football with me again, which was understandable. But she also said that she forgave me, and that she was proud of me. *What!* I thought. She said she was proud of me for understanding why my actions would hurt her and for taking responsibility. She told me I was a good man.

Those words spoke directly to my soul. It felt like that moment in the movie *How the Grinch Stole Christmas* where his heart grew three sizes because of the love he experienced through the people of Whoville.

I was good. I wasn't bad. Stefanie chose to speak life into me and to speak the truth about me. My actions were bad, but I wasn't. And this angel of a woman made that very clear to me. It truly changed my life, and I felt so free in that moment—like I could conquer any giant, run to the top of any mountain peak, or dunk a basketball from anywhere on the court.

THE POWER OF TRUTH

As you can see from Caleb's story, truth has the ability to pierce through a moment of frustration and pain. Believing the truth is a game changer that allows you to stop the toxic thoughts and cycles in their tracks. It brings you one step closer to your goal of finding healing from past pain or trauma so you can experience the wholehearted love God intended for you.

Though Stefanie was every bit justified in pointing out the wrong, it was the truth spoken in that moment that had the power to change the course of our relationship. As we move forward in this chapter, take special notice of how truth changes other situations. You'll see how to apply it immediately when you are believing toxic thoughts. Developing this skill can change your life. It has taken some practice, but the two of us have learned so much about letting truth rule over our toxic thoughts, and you can do this too, friend. There is light at the end of the tunnel.

Decorating our Christmas tree is one of our favorite traditions in the holiday season. We make it an event. After moving to Pittsburgh, we went to a Christmas tree farm about twenty minutes away from our house to pick out a tree. It was an experience seeing all the different shapes and sizes available, and it was fun to pick out and take home our favorite. We even got to chop it down ourselves!

At home, we have an awesome process for putting it all together, as well as a specific look we go for. The lights go on first, then some gold and white artificial flowers, and we finish it off with the ornaments and the star at the top.

Have you ever put the lights on a tree? It can be tricky. Of course, the first time you use them, they work perfectly. But if you reuse your lights the next year, you have to make sure they all still work. If one bulb is burnt out, the rest of them after it on the strand won't work either.

You have to trace back to the one that's out and change it so the rest will light up properly. If some of the lights are burnt out, it's not going to look good, and it could be a fire hazard as well. Once you locate a new bulb to fit the strand, it will work the way it was intended to. Now you can have a beautiful, bright Christmas tree for the entire holiday season.

Tracing back to the source of our toxic thoughts is kind of like finding the troublesome Christmas light. When you are feeling triggered by a situation—maybe someone calls you a name or yells at you, or you see your ex—and you find yourself coping to get through it, you have to trace your feelings back to the source. You need to find the original toxic thought about yourself and replace it with the truth. This will allow you to break those old cycles and start living in new ways—ways that are much more like what you have always dreamed of.

TRUTHS TO REPLACE TOXIC THOUGHTS

Let's go back to Sarah from chapter 4. If you remember, she had made a mistake at work, and her boss reprimanded her about her performance, so she felt like a failure.

What if instead of blaming, yelling, and withdrawing, Sarah recognized her toxic thought, and said to herself, *I'm feeling like a failure right now, but what's the truth? What do I need to tell myself? I made a mistake but that doesn't mean that I am a mistake. When I make a mistake, that means I can do better next time. Everyone makes mistakes. That doesn't mean I am not loved. I am loved.*

Do you think the rest of her workday would have gone better? Maybe she wouldn't have gotten into such an argument with Fred later that night.

We have all been there in those moments, oftentimes without realizing what is really going on. The good news is that you can train your mind to recognize when you are about to get upset and go into a toxic cycle. You can replace the toxic thought with the truth, calm down, and feel okay again.

A great way to think about it is to consider what you would tell your best friend in the same situation. How would you encourage them? When you realize that you can say the same things to yourself, it allows you to get unstuck. You can emotionally connect to yourself so that you can start speaking that truth over your concerns. You can treat yourself the same way you would treat your best friend. You might even need to tell yourself to cool down and give yourself grace.

Believing what God says can stop a toxic cycle in its tracks.

But what is the truth that we need to speak over ourselves? What do we replace the toxic thoughts with?

The *truth* is believing what God says about you, about others, and about Himself. Speaking the truth over the toxic cycle can stop it in its tracks before it can do you more harm or pour over into your relationships with others.

What we tell ourselves in a moment of pain will significantly impact the rest of our day and the days to come. Are we telling ourselves something based on how we feel? Or are we stopping to let God's love meet us in our deepest areas of hurt? Every toxic thought that we struggle with can be directly combated with truth from God's Word.

Following are three lists of common toxic thoughts you may experience about yourself, about others, and about God—and the truth from God's Word that you can replace them with. Any time you find yourself believing one of these toxic thoughts, you can come back to these verses and remind yourself of what God says is true. Take some time to read through these lists and note the ones that sound familiar.

TOXIC THOUGHTS ABOUT *YOURSELF*
VS. THE TRUTH FROM GOD'S WORD

Toxic Thought	God's Truth
I'm not good enough	I was chosen by God | Eph. 1:4
I'm unloved	I am loved by God | Rom. 8:35-39
I'm unworthy	Jesus loves me like God loves Him | John 15:9
I'm worthless	I am valuable to God | Matt. 6:26
I'm alone	I am never alone | Deut. 31:8
I am rejected	I am chosen by God | 1 Pet. 2:9
I am set aside	I am set apart by God | John 17:15-18
I'm a failure	I am strengthened for all tasks to which God calls me | Phil. 4:13
I have no purpose in life	I have a purpose | Jer. 29:11
I am unsafe	I have been rescued | Col. 1:13
Others are better than me	I have value too | Mark 12:30-31
I'm ugly	I am wonderfully made | Psalm 139:14
I'm not gifted	I have unique gifts | Rom. 12:6-21
I'm unlovable	I am called by God | Rom. 8.20, 30
I'm an object	I am God's handiwork | Eph. 2:10
I'm an embarrassment	I am set apart for good things | Jer. 1:5
My voice doesn't matter	When I speak, God is with me | Acts 18:9-10
I'm a mistake	God created me | Psalm 139:13
My past defines me	I am a new creation | Gal. 2:20 I am not condemned | Rom. 8:1
I won't have enough	God will meet my needs | Phil. 4:19
I am weak	I am strengthened for all tasks to which God calls me | Phil. 4:13
My body should be used and abused	My body is where the Holy Spirit abides | 1 Cor. 6:19; John 14:16

TOXIC THOUGHTS ABOUT *OTHERS*
VS. THE TRUTH FROM GOD'S WORD

Toxic Thought	God's Truth
They are worthless	Jesus loves them like God loves Him | John 15:9
They don't matter	They are valuable to God | Matt. 6:26
They are an object	They are God's handiwork | Eph. 2:10
They have no purpose	God has given them a purpose | Jer. 29:11
I am better than them	Others are valued by God too | Phil. 2:3-4

TOXIC THOUGHTS ABOUT *GOD*
VS. THE TRUTH FROM GOD'S WORD

Toxic Thought	God's Truth
God doesn't love me	I am a child of God | John 1:12
God isn't good	God is good | Psalm 34:8
God doesn't care	Jesus prays for me | John 17:9; Heb. 7:25 God has rescued me | Col. 1:13
God is holding out on me	God doesn't want to withhold any good thing from me | Psalm 84:11
God isn't looking out for me	God sent Jesus to die for me | John 3:16 I am a gift to Jesus from God | John 17:9, 12, 14
I don't belong with God	I have been brought into the Kingdom and eternal life | Col. 1:13
God doesn't listen to me	I have access to God through Jesus | Eph. 2:18; 3:12 I am called by God | Rom. 8:28, 30
God wants to steal my fun	God gives me abundant life | John 10:10
Life ends when I die	I have everlasting life | John 6:47
God will always condemn me	I am forgiven | Col. 2:13-14 I am not condemned | Rom. 8:1
Following God will be boring	I have peace with God through Jesus | Rom. 5:1

STEFANIE'S STORY: WHO ARE YOU, REALLY?

When my fiancé Todd dumped me on Valentine's Day, I lost so much more than just that relationship. It was less than two years earlier that I had made a commitment to go all in with Jesus. Around the same time, I started dating Todd and doing ministry with him every moment I could.

I thought I knew what my future was going to look like, but now I didn't. I thought I knew who my friends were, but they all chose to stay with Todd (since he was their boss). My family loved me, but they hadn't been fans of all my changes the last two years. I had friends from before I was a Christian, but the drinking and nightly parties were no longer things that gave me peace. I had always been a good student and was several months away from graduating at the time of the breakup, but I missed some assignments and felt like I was failing at that too.

I had put my identity in my family, my romantic relationship, my friendships, my ministry work, and school. And in an instant, all of those identities had been taken from me.

I was stunned. I was broken beyond anything I'd experienced before. But God came to my rescue. Penn State is a huge campus, and as I walked between classes, I listened to the song "Praise You in This Storm" on repeat:

And I'll praise You in this storm
And I will lift my hands
For You are who You are
No matter where I am
And every tear I've cried
You hold in Your hand
You never left my side
And though my heart is torn
I will praise You in this storm[1]

That was my heart's anthem. He was who He was no matter what.

Psalm 18:2 and many other verses became real like never before. "The LORD is my rock, my fortress and my deliverer; my God is my rock, in whom I take refuge, my shield and the horn of my salvation, my stronghold."

Although the storm in my heart was big, and I was lying without strength on a rock, that Rock was a firm foundation. My own strength was gone, but He became my strength. My dreams were dead, but He gave hope back to me. My identity was shattered, and He started teaching me who I really was without all the facades and nonsense that I thought made me important. I cried out to God a lot. I felt lost and confused. But I had an overwhelming peace that choosing Him over anything of the world was my only option. And I wasn't going to look back.

God came to my rescue in some unexpected ways. At church, I heard about a mission trip to New Orleans to help people who had been impacted by Hurricane Katrina four years earlier. It was through a Christian ministry at our college called the Navigators. Finally, here was a group of people who didn't answer to Todd. My spirit was revived by the thought of being involved in ministry again.

On the trip, talking with some of the new girls I was meeting was a breath of fresh air. I didn't know anyone before the trip, but they were all kind, welcoming, and loving toward me. At night, all the women stayed in one big room, with our sleeping bags spread out all over the place, and we sat and talked for hours. I met girls named Emily, Paige, and Maggie who showed me extraordinary kindness. Emily had also gone through a really rough breakup in her past. She knew what it was like to be mistreated, but she wasn't playing the victim. Instead, she talked from an empowered point of view.

She was attentive when I told her about my broken engagement. She wasn't judgmental, but spoke kindly, compassionately,
and with so much tenderness. I shared things with her that I
hadn't yet been able to process, even with my therapist. When
I divulged details from my past, she affirmed that they weren't
right and that they shouldn't have happened to me. She was so
sorry I had gone through that much pain. She assured me that
God would hold me through all of it and that there was hope
on the other side.

My heart softened during those days on the mission trip.
Glimmers of hope started streaming through my soul. I had
expressed to the women my anxious thoughts about where I would
live after May, since I would no longer be getting married and
moving into my fiancé's condo. I had nowhere to go. Paige told
me about a house she and some of the other women were going to
live in. She invited me to join them.

WOW! God showed up big on that trip. The toxic thoughts of
Your life is over, *No one will love you anymore*, and *There's no purpose
for you* were being drowned out by God's amazing truth.

Senior year ended and I moved my things into the beautiful
home I was renting with the five other women. I had brought
everything from my old apartment but something felt "off." For
some reason, I didn't have the energy to unpack or hang up my
clothes.

I broke down in tears. *What's going on, God?* I asked.

As I looked at my things, a light bulb went off in my head.
Who are you, really?

Holding up one shirt, I thought back to my motivation
in buying it: I wanted to look sexy to get a guy's attention.
I pulled out my "Love Spell" perfume: my desire had been to
put a "spell" on men so I could cover my pain of being *not good
enough*. I looked at my football posters: I had invested so much

time into the Steelers, and I loved that it made me a "cool" girl in front of the boys. But did I even like the sport? I looked at my CDs: Did I really like these artists, or was I just listening to them to fit in?

I realized so many of my things were bought to cope with toxic thoughts. I had been trying to get approval from others and to be good enough in their eyes. I couldn't put anything away because I wasn't willing to put on these masks one more day. I prayed,

God, I have no idea who I really am. All my life, all my actions have been an effort to be good enough to get love from others. But I don't want that anymore. I want to know who You say I am. I'm here, my life and possessions poured out before You. I only want to be who You've made me to be. I want to let go of everything else.

I didn't know it then, but God had started to reveal His truth to me. I felt Him tell me that He loves me, that I am His child. I took that knowledge and held it close to my heart. And I sorted through my belongings with God, giving to charity all the clothes that no longer served me in this new season. My remaining wardrobe was small, but my heart was filled with hope.

God was teaching me the truth about my identity, His identity, and the identity of others in a way that was setting me free. Nothing that I had done to fill my empty places ever satisfied before. And now my heart was being filled with an unshakable love that was giving me undeniable peace.

THE TRUTH THAT SATISFIES

In our search for truth, what better person than Jesus to tell us what will truly satisfy the longing of our hearts? John 4 tells us of an encounter He had with a Samaritan woman who had been searching for truth and identity. It was about noon when Jesus saw her come to draw water at Jacob's well. The woman was shocked when Jesus—a Jew—asked her—a Samaritan—for a drink. In their culture, Jews didn't associate with Samaritans.

The woman was puzzled about why He would ask her for water. Jesus responded, "If you knew the gift of God and who it is that asks you for a drink, you would have asked him and he would have given you living water" (verse 10).

She questioned this response, and Jesus told her, "Everyone who drinks this water will be thirsty again, but whoever drinks the water I give them will never thirst. Indeed, the water I give them will become in them a spring of water welling up to eternal life" (verses 13 and 14).

Of course, the woman wanted *this* water! She thought it meant she wouldn't have to keep coming to the well in the heat of the day.

Jesus started telling the Samaritan woman things about herself that He could not have known. He knew that she had no husband now, but that she'd had five husbands in the past. He knew that the man she was with now was not her husband.

The well of this Samaritan woman's soul was dry. She had been desperately trying to overcome her toxic thoughts and fill her need for worth with husband after husband. She had been attempting to get her validation from a male's attention and affection. But each time, she came up empty. Jesus was offering her the chance for her soul to be quenched in a way she had never experienced—to be fully known, seen, loved, and forgiven, and to have the joy of eternal life, and life right now to the full.

We all have a desire to be fully known, loved, and seen. Our love tank must be filled. And when we don't know the right places to fill it, we will run to anything and everything to meet our needs. But God wants to satisfy us with His truth. He wants to meet us in our empty and broken places and in our heartbreak and show us how truly loved we are.

Have you been looking for your worth in a well that keeps running dry? The two of us have experienced this, and so did the Samaritan woman. But God wants to fill our soul with living water that will never run out.

Do you remember when we talked about how our toxic thoughts go on autopilot? In the preceding chapters we encouraged you to start "thinking about what you are thinking about." God wants to pave new paths for our brain. He wants to exchange toxic thoughts for the truth so we are filled with His peace.

Jesus wants to meet you in your deepest pain and speak a new identity over each toxic thought. Will you let Him?

Jesus wants to meet you in your deepest areas of pain and speak a new identity over each and every toxic thought. Will you let Him?

Knowing how to apply the truth changes everything. As we have seen in this chapter, the truth quite literally sets us free. So what happens when we learn to act in the truth in our everyday lives? It allows us to be the most beautiful version of ourselves. In the next chapter we will explore more deeply how we can act in the truth we now know about who God says we are and what Jesus did for us. Then, we will see how to start applying those principles immediately.

MAKING IT PERSONAL

Scripture to Apply

We invite you to read the verses below. Take notice of the special care God displays for you in Scripture, and how it makes you feel to read these truths. Summarize what you see in these verses in the space provided below.

The very hairs of your head are all numbered. Don't be afraid; you are worth more than many sparrows. (Luke 12:7)

It is by grace you have been saved, through faith—and this is not from yourselves, it is the gift of God—not by works, so that no one can boast. For we are God's handiwork, created in Christ Jesus to do good works, which God prepared in advance for us to do. (Ephesians 2:8-10)

This is what the LORD says—he who created you, Jacob, he who formed you, Israel: "Do not fear, for I have redeemed you; I have summoned you by name; you are mine." (Isaiah 43:1)

Look at the birds of the air; they do not sow or reap or store away in barns, and yet your heavenly Father feeds them. Are you not much more valuable than they? (Matthew 6:26)

God created mankind in his own image, in the image of God he created them; male and female he created them. . . . God saw all that he had made, and it was very good. And there was evening, and there was morning—the sixth day. (Genesis 1:27, 31)

Here are a few additional verses you may wish to look up if you have time: Psalm 84:11; Jeremiah 2:13; John 4:10; John 7:38; Galatians 2:20; Colossians 1:14.

Questions to Consider

1. In what areas of your life have you felt empty?

2. Where have you been getting your identity? (For example, this could be relationships, your financial status, attention from others, skills, your work, or activities.)

3. Review the lists of truths over toxic thoughts earlier in this chapter. Which one do you most need to hold on to this week to replace toxic thoughts?

Call to Action

Sit with Jesus in your area of pain. Ask Him to show you how He sees you. Ask God where He was in that moment of pain. Ask Him to retell your story in light of His perspective.

Write down several of the truths from God's Word (see the tables earlier in this chapter) on sticky notes and meditate on those words over your identity. Each time you become aware of a toxic thought coming up this week, try to replace it with one of these truths. Speak His truth out loud any time you feel anxious, overwhelmed, or sad.

8

Acting in Truth

CHOOSING TO TAKE POSITIVE STEPS
BASED ON GOD'S WORD

CALEB'S STORY: THE DAY TIME STOOD STILL

"WHO IS THAT!"

My "whispered" question to my friend Sara nearly broke her eardrum, but I had just seen an angel.

"Her?" Sara said, pointing across the sanctuary. "That's Stef Stack."

Jaw dropping to the floor, I replied, "I have to get to know her!"

I'll never forget that first time I laid eyes on Stefanie. Now, I know what you're thinking: *Caleb, there is no such thing as love at first sight.* But I beg to differ. Whatever it was that I experienced, it changed me forever.

But let's step back a few months. As I mentioned earlier, I was working as a substitute teacher and basketball coach while completing my master's degree. I was also still trying to find the right person for me, but I had almost lost hope. I told myself, *If I start looking everywhere, eventually I will find her.* I began to walk that out in my life, frequenting clubs, bars, and churches (funny that I included those together). I was desperate and looking to fill a void only God could fill.

I had a list of requirements for my dream girl: good-looking, funny, Christian, active, likes sports, to name a few. I could find people who fit some of those wants but not all of them, so I would set my standards lower. Eventually, the only remaining require-ment, really, was that she be female.

Wow, had my standards dropped. I finally realized it was time for a change.

First, I had to address the core toxic thought that I was believ-ing: *God doesn't love me, and He no longer has a meaningful purpose for my life.* I had decided I was on my own, and I was going to have to settle for second best.

Then I had to replace that toxic thought with the truth: *God loves me beyond measure.* That is, there is no sense of earthly mea-sure that can approach the amount of love that God has for me. On top of that, *He has an amazing purpose for my life.* I knew that only when I believed those truths would I find the healing and restoration that I needed.

So, I chose to submit this dream to Him, letting go of my control over any future marriage.

As you might already have figured out, submitting things to God doesn't happen overnight. You can't expect to immediately release something you've held on to so closely. It took practice, it took daily sacrifice, but while the desire for a life partner was still in me, it didn't consume me like before. That allowed me to have more time and energy for other things I enjoyed and for building a career.

During those years after college, I had tried a few different churches until I landed at one in Eagle Rock, California. I always went to the Sunday evening service since it was geared toward young adults. There was a hangout across the street, with a coffee shop and live music provided by the church, where people could connect after the service. It was a fun atmosphere, and I loved being able to go with my friends, hear God's Word, and interact with others my age. I enjoyed the overall vibe, but I had never met anyone there that I was interested in.

But then came the night everything changed.

Spotlight from Heaven

I walked into the sanctuary as usual, but as I got to my seat, I looked across the room to my left. And there was Stefanie. In that moment, I am convinced that time stopped.

Have you ever seen the movie *Big Fish*? It has some amazing visual effects, including one of my favorite scenes ever because I relate to it so much. The main character walks into a circus where there is a ton of action going on—people performing with fire, acrobats flying through the air. In his scan of the room, he sees a girl, and the narrator comments, "They say when you meet the love of your life, time stops, and that's true."

As he says this, all motion stops, and it's like there is a spotlight on the woman. The young man is enamored of her beauty and radiance. He walks between the circus performers as they are paused in time, until he gets to her. It's an amazing portrayal of what it feels like to be struck by love at first sight. And it's exactly how it felt for me.

It was as if there were a spotlight from heaven on Stefanie. She was wearing a beautiful sundress, and she shone like a beam of light in the room. I was captivated by her every movement. Within seconds, I was head over heels for her. I knew she hadn't noticed me (even though I'm six-foot-five and stick out like a sore thumb) because she was fully engaged in the worship of her Savior. I feel like I saw Stefanie that day in the fullest, purest version of who God created her to be.

After the service, I practically sprinted to the hangout across the street, and eventually, I built up the courage to go over and talk to her. Because, let's be honest, how do you talk to someone who looks like an angel? But I did. I walked up to her, and I asked her to marry me, and we lived happily ever after . . .

I *wish* that was how it went.

But in reality, I introduced myself, and within two seconds this DUDE walks up, puts his arm around her, and says, "What's up, man?"

It was like he owned her. My heart sank to my feet, and being the nonconfrontational person I am, I said, "My name's Caleb. So nice to meet you." Then I walked away.

Now, for most people, it might have ended there. But for me, this was the beginning. That night, I gave Stefanie the nickname "Dream Girl," and I promised myself that if she was ever available again, I would go after her.

I knew I wasn't ready for a woman like that, as much as I wished I could be. But this was an opportunity to put into practice what I had been learning. I had to submit "Dream Girl" to God. I spent the next year bettering myself, growing in my relationship with God, and finishing my master's degree.

I assumed that Stefanie would probably marry that guy because of how he acted around her. It seemed like he had her locked up. I had to let it go. As hard as it was for me, I decided that I couldn't control it, and God would take care of me. I knew that Stefanie deserved to be married to someone good who would treat her right, and I felt like I didn't deserve a woman like her. But if God willed it, He could make it happen.

Making Good on a Promise

Almost a year later, I went on a mission trip to Nicaragua with the school where I had been working. We would take students down to do upkeep on a missionary property and to coordinate fun activities for the neighborhood kids.

High school students want to know everything about you and your personal life. I got asked so many times if I was dating anyone. Finally, I told them about "Dream Girl," who was amazing, breathtaking, and everything I wanted in a life partner. The students were enthralled with my story and made me promise that if she was ever unattached again, I would ask her out right away. That was a Friday, and we headed back to the States on Saturday.

On Sunday, I walked into church expecting to go to the service as usual. I might see Stefanie, say a meek little "hello" and move on. But no . . . when I opened the door, Stefanie caught my eye immediately because, well, she was "Dream Girl." Usually we didn't really talk, but I saw her coming toward me, and she said, "Hey, Caleb!"

I was shocked, but I fully enjoyed that moment. We talked for a bit and she invited me to the church's Fourth of July picnic. I said yes because there is no other answer to give Stefanie. And she walked away, saying, "See you around."

My friend Sara came up to me and said, "Did you hear?"

"Hear what?"

"Stef is *single!*" It was like the song "Celebration" had come on over the speakers. I wanted to do my most outrageous happy dance right then and there. I had thought things were serious with her boyfriend and that I had zero chance—only a hope and a prayer. But she was available again!

After that, I got extremely nervous every time I saw her. It wasn't easy to talk to her or open up. I was terrified that I might mess this up. So I enlisted my friend Sara to befriend Stefanie and organize hangouts together as a group so that we could get to know each other better.

I take a while to warm up, and I can be a little shy at first, so it took some time. But by the grace of God, I was eventually able to be myself around her.

One night we had a group get-together at the Rose Bowl Stadium, which has a three-mile trail around it. We walked the trail, laughing and cracking jokes, and I got to share with Stefanie more of my heart for God and for student ministries. I felt like I could open up to her more than to anyone else. I remember walking next to her, and every so often our shoulders would bump. It gave me goose bumps and sent me soaring! I was on cloud nine, and the woman of my dreams was with me.

I called her the next day and asked her out, and we went on our first date the following Thursday. It was magical, and I fell head over heels in love that summer of 2012 with that beautiful, brown-eyed girl. This last decade since then, we've hardly spent time apart because I can never get enough of her.

CHOOSING TO ACT IN THE TRUTH

We have covered so many things together in this book, from identifying toxic thoughts to learning how to replace them with the truth. But the thing is, you can recognize them and replace them, but then what do you do? The next step toward finding healing from past pain or trauma so we can experience wholehearted love as God intended is to *act* in the truth.

We all have so many moments when we can make a choice. We can choose to believe the toxic thoughts that inevitably come up, or we can choose something different. It takes a lot of practice to be able to do that effectively. But when we do, it is a freeing feeling.

Acting in the truth is living out of abundance. We aren't reacting in pain. We aren't trying to earn our worth. Instead, we are acting in our true identity with peace and confidence.

That night I (Caleb) first met Stefanie, I felt something different. I felt that I had just met "my person." And quite honestly, it didn't really go my way that night. That dude blew me off. And in that moment, I had a choice: Was I going to believe the toxic thoughts *I am not good enough, I don't deserve someone like Stefanie,* and *God doesn't have a plan for me*? Or, was I going to choose something different, something better?

Looking back, I am so proud I chose to do something different. Stefanie was the girl I had waited for my entire life, and I didn't want to lose out on her. But by learning from my experiences in life—my dead dream, my lost job, and others—I was able to give my love life fully to God, even when I had met the person I wanted the most.

Is submitting ourselves to God a guarantee that He is going to fulfill our every dream? Granted, not everyone's story falls into place the way ours did. But one thing we can tell you for sure: if you give your future over to God, including your possible future spouse, the life He provides for you will be more rewarding and fulfilling than you could ever arrange for yourself.

That year that I waited and prepared for Stefanie wasn't full of hurt, pain, self-pity, and toxic cycles, as it easily could have been. It was full of trust, hope, and belief that God had something good waiting for me. And it encouraged me to grow into the type of man Stefanie deserved.

When we choose to act in the truth, we choose to believe something true over ourselves.

Think about David in the Old Testament. Can you imagine how the story of his battle with Goliath would have gone if he had believed the toxic thoughts spoken over him by others as well as the ones that very likely went through his own brain? I mean, Goliath was *huge*, bigger than any man David had ever seen before, a mighty warrior. The greatest in the army of Israel practically peed their pants over this guy. And do you blame them?

I can't say I would have been like David at that moment.

When bringing supplies to the battle line, David overheard Goliath taunting the Israelites. He also heard the reward for defeating the giant—wealth and the king's daughter's hand in marriage. David inquired about this, but his brother said to him, "Who did you leave those few sheep with in the wilderness? I know your arrogance and your evil heart—you came down to see the battle!" (1 Samuel 17:28, CSB).

That hurts. When someone close to us speaks like this, it causes us to feel awful about ourselves. It's easy to let toxic thoughts come in under these circumstances.

But it doesn't stop there. Saul heard about David's inquiries and called him in to speak with him. Saul said, "You can't go fight this Philistine. You're just a youth, and he's been a warrior since he was young" (1 Samuel 17:33, CSB).

Do you hear the toxic thoughts pouring in? *You're evil. You're arrogant. You're too young. You're not good enough. You can't do this.*

All of these statements pointed directly to the core of who David was and what his purpose was. At this moment, David's purpose was laid on the line, and God's future promise to him was at stake (see 2 Samuel 7:5-16). David was faced with the same decision that many of us face in these moments: Do we choose to believe the toxic thoughts, or do we decide to act in truth?

David chose to act in truth. He immediately responded that he had taken down lions and bears, and that in the same way, he could strike down this Philistine who was speaking against God. He chose to act in the full knowledge that God was with him, like He always had been.

We all know how this story ends. David slew Goliath and eventually became king of Israel. David claimed what God had in store for him, not in his own strength but in the truth of who he was and who God created him to be.

At what moments in your life have you chosen to act in truth? At what moments have you chosen to believe toxic thoughts?

TAKING OUR THOUGHTS CAPTIVE

Looking back at the story of David, we can't say we would have blamed him for leaving the battlefield scared that day. He would have been justified; Goliath was a beast. But instead, David's story was recorded in God's Word, and he has been famous throughout history because of his choice to act in truth.

It makes us think of all the opportunities God has given us to make that same choice in difficult situations and to act on what the Bible says. We've told you about many of the times we believed toxic thoughts over God's truth. But God gives us new opportunities daily to choose Him over what we are facing.

Your spouse is frustrated with how you folded the laundry and spews out mean words toward you. Do you choose to spew back? Or do you claim the truth and choose forgiveness and humility instead?

Your friends call you names behind your back and you hear them one day. Do you believe those toxic thoughts and give in to self-pity and despair? Or do you choose to know what God says about you? Do you choose to walk forward in confidence with Him, finding better friends in the future?

These choices are scattered throughout our days, and we hope that seeing how we can change our mindset will give you strength and power in those moments to choose the truth and act in it.

Seeing how we can change our mindset gives us strength and power to choose the truth and act in it.

The apostle Paul tells us that we need to "demolish arguments and every pretension that sets itself up against the knowledge of God, and . . . take captive every thought to make it obedient to Christ" (2 Corinthians 10:5).

As we pave new trails in our brain, our tendency is to go back to our old thought patterns. We want to encourage you to keep thinking about what you're thinking about. Be attuned to what triggers you and be diligent in taking captive any thought that isn't in line with God's truth. Then you will be in a good place to act in that truth.

What exactly does acting in the truth look like? Here are ways that we act when we are connected to the truth of God:

POSITIVE ACTIONS:[1]

Help others in an appropriate way.
Be present.
Have conversations.
Show patience.
Exhibit openness.
Be self-aware.
Act confidently.
Stay focused.
Work hard.
Maintain healthy boundaries.
Get a healthy amount of exercise.
Eat a healthy diet.
Strive for financial peace and wise decisions.
Be happy for others.
Be satisfied with life.
Be willing to grow.

God has a great purpose for you, just like He did for David. Our prayer is that you choose to walk in that purpose, knowing that He loves you and that He *will* give you the strength to do it.

Whether it's the desire to get married or to be a better spouse or to help other people—whatever God has put in your life, He will empower you to accomplish it through His strength. The only person who can get in the way of God's plan for your life is you.

STEFANIE'S STORY: REDEEMING THE BROKENNESS

It was four years from the day I sat in the middle of my room, clothes and possessions around me, asking God who I really was and asking Him to show me how to truly be who He created me to be. Not the Stefanie that everyone else expected of me. Not the Stefanie that would get me more attention. Just me. No masks. No filters. No facades.

God was teaching me to throw off my old ways of coping. Instead of treating men as objects, I was learning to honor them. To see them as people made in His image. To treat them with respect—not leading them on, not playing games, and not using them to fill my love tank. I was going to God for my worth now, so I was able to treat others around me with way more love and respect than I had ever been able to previously.

I no longer felt like a victim of my past abuse and pain. I was no longer in a self-pity and self-preservation mode. I felt empowered by Jesus with the right "armor" to see who was safe for me and who wasn't. I didn't entertain things that didn't give me peace. I made decisions with much more confidence because I was trusting God to lead. I was hearing His voice more than ever before because I was spending the time listening to Him each morning and I carried that throughout the day.

Dating had looked so different in those last four years. My toxic thoughts of *I'm not good enough* and *I'm unlovable* were being met by Jesus, and He was filling my life. I was now allowing my unquenchable thirst for attention and admiration to be met (most of the time) by God.

In the past, I would have dated people out of these toxic thoughts and a scarcity mindset: *You better stay with him. You won't find anyone better. At least he gives you attention.* Now, I was no longer making decisions in relationships to keep someone in my life who had no business being there in the first place.

My old toxic thoughts of *I have to lower my boundaries sexually so he will stay* or *I don't need to show self-control because I need to know I am loved* were turning into *I get to have self-control because God created my body to be a temple of the Holy Spirit. I want to honor God with my body. A man who respects me will respect the boundaries I set. I don't need to be physical with a man in order to know I am loved. I don't need to lower my boundaries to keep someone around.*

When I dated men out of a love tank that was already being filled by God, I could date with intention and wisdom. I used to think I was courageous to go on a date with anyone who showed me interest. But I started to realize that courage without wisdom was stupidity. God cared about leading me in the small ways of my life. How much more did He care about who I was going to spend my life with? I surrendered this area to Him, trusting Him with it so I could go into dating with peace, clarity, and freedom.

When I met Caleb, I'd never experienced someone so genuine. Hanging out with him was different than with anyone else I'd ever been around. He was kind, compassionate, and funny, and he had a big heart for God and others. As we started going on dates, I felt so free to be my full self around him. I had no desire to put a mask back on, and that was something I was unwilling to compromise on. Masks are exhausting.

With each date we had, I felt a peace that surpassed understanding. Being with him made me feel more alive. I'd never felt more seen, more known, and more loved by a man before.

Several months into our dating relationship, Caleb invited me to walk on the beach with him. He picked me up in his red 1997 Ford Explorer—the car we had all our adventures in. We sang many songs at the top of our lungs as we danced in our seats on the way to the beach. We talked, laughed, and shared stories about our pasts. We felt so safe, and we felt God's smile on us as we were together. There is no one in the world more funny to me than Caleb. I laughed harder, smiled more, and felt more loved than ever before.

As we walked along the beach holding hands, we told each other how special it was that we felt this way about each other. Caleb told me, "I love you, Stefanie."

"I love you, Caleb." I stood on tiptoe, sand beneath my feet, as we hugged, while the sun lowered over the ocean at Crystal Cove Beach.

On the way home, we listened to a song by Matthew West as I thanked God.

> *There must be a God, I believe it's true*
> *'Cause I can see His love, when I look at you*
> *And He must have a plan for this crazy life*
> *Because He brought you here and placed you by my side*[2]

Listening to these lyrics, I could feel God's redemption. He was redeeming all those years of brokenness before my very eyes.

Several months later, on that very same beach, Caleb got down on one knee and asked me to be his wife. I had thought I would be terrified the next time I got engaged (if that was even going to happen for me again). But here I was, with the man of my dreams kneeling before me. There was even a big rainbow over his head. I cried and yelled in excitement, saying, "YES, YES, YES!" I praised Jesus for His promises and love that were better than I could have imagined.

On our wedding day, I walked down the aisle to the Matthew West song. This love story God had given me was worth all the tears, all the years of pain, and I could feel His love when I looked at Caleb.

JESUS, OUR PRIME EXAMPLE

Whatever pain you're holding today, God isn't done with your story. Just as He has done for us, He wants to "repay you for the years the locusts have eaten" (Joel 2:25). He wants to bring redemption to your heart. He wants to lavish His love on you like never before. Whatever dreams feel dead or broken, He can make new. He made your heart and He knows its desires. He has a plan for you, and He wants to fill your life with good things. Do you believe this? Do you want to believe this more today?

Often, it's hard to picture what living wholeheartedly and loving wholeheartedly could look like. It can feel like traveling a trail without a map, thinking you are making the right turns, but sometimes finding yourself in a place you never expected to be.

Jesus always acts in truth, and He is the embodiment of wholehearted love.

As we look for ways to love more wholeheartedly and to act in the truth, our prime example is in the actions and life of Jesus. He always acts in truth, and He is the embodiment of wholehearted love.

Let's look at several characteristics of Jesus that enable Him to love wholeheartedly and that we can start putting into practice today.

Jesus knows His identity and fixes His eyes on His Father.

Jesus had many haters. A lot of people labeled Him. But He walked His days on earth knowing *who* He was and *whose* He was. He didn't let others' words define Him but clung to His identity as God's "beloved Son" (Matthew 3:17, csb). No matter what was going on around Him, He kept His eyes on the Father and never lost sight of His purpose. The writer of Hebrews tells us to keep our eyes fixed on Jesus as our example because "for the joy set before him he endured the cross, scorning its shame, and sat down at the right hand of the throne of God." He "endured such opposition from sinners" and kept His focus on heaven (12:2-3).

So how do we put this into practice throughout our week? Throughout our lives? Focus on what God says about you and on the voices of truth in your life. Philippians 4:8 tells us, "Whatever is true, whatever is noble, whatever is right, whatever is pure, whatever is lovely, whatever is admirable—if anything is excellent or praiseworthy—think about such things." Focus on the ways God has showed up in your life. Focus on the good, right things. Instead of fixating on your circumstance, consider how God could be using it for good. Set your eyes on heaven. Meditate on the fact that God has already won the war. During the battles you face this week, you can praise Him for the ultimate victory.

When your true identity is what you cling to and speak over your life most, your thirst is satisfied by the true source. Trying to gratify your insatiable desire for attention and affirmation with things in this world will prove futile. Only the love of Jesus will fulfill the deep longings of your soul.

Fear and doubt can get in the way of achieving your goals. Thinking *This isn't going to work for me* will zap your energy. Reframe this negative thought to *God has brought me to this place because He wants to make a breakthrough in my life. This time it can be different. God is for me and not against me.*

PUT IT INTO PRACTICE·

Choose thankfulness.
Find ways to see and thank God.
Accept winning in relationships as reality.
Choose to see the victory to come.
Focus on the things unseen.

Live in the reality that your relationship goals aren't that far
out of reach.

Start acting like God's child now; you are so loved and
cherished.

Be resourceful instead of giving up on your goals.

Take out the old tape and start playing a new one right now.

Change *I am unlovable* and *I'm going to feel alone forever* to *I
will feel connected.*

Jesus gets His purpose and worth from the right source.

Jesus came to this earth for a purpose: to show us the life we should
live, to die the death that was meant for us. He was the sinless one
taking on the debt of all the guilty, and this was God's purpose for
Him before we even knew it. Paul tells us that "God demonstrates
his own love for us in this: While we were still sinners, Christ died for
us. Since we have now been justified by his blood, how much more
shall we be saved from God's wrath through him!" (Romans 5:8-9).

Jesus didn't stray from His mission even when it grew difficult,
but depended fully on God to help Him fulfill it:

> During the days of Jesus' life on earth, he offered up
> prayers and petitions with fervent cries and tears to the
> one who could save him from death, and he was heard
> because of his reverent submission. Son though he was,
> he learned obedience from what he suffered and, once
> made perfect, he became the source of eternal salvation
> for all who obey him.
>
> HEBREWS 5:7-9

Jesus never doubted what He came to do. He knew His purpose and worth came from God alone, and He fixed His eyes
constantly on God. And remember, we are made in the image of

our Creator. God has an amazing purpose for our lives as well, as we follow Jesus' example:

> In your relationships with one another, have the same
> mindset as Christ Jesus: Who, being in very nature God,
> did not consider equality with God something to be used
> to his own advantage; rather, he made himself nothing by
> taking the very nature of a servant, being made in human
> likeness. And being found in appearance as a man, he
> humbled himself by becoming obedient to death—even
> death on a cross! Therefore God exalted him to the highest
> place and gave him the name that is above every name.
> PHILIPPIANS 2:5-9

God wants us to live, love, and walk in Jesus' footsteps—to walk with purpose to bring the Kingdom of Heaven to this earth. Knowing God has entrusted us with such a purpose should give us a great sense of worth.

PUT IT INTO PRACTICE:
Know that God has a good purpose for your life.
Know that just as parents see the best version of their child,
    God sees the best version of you.
Remember that God sees you the way He sees Jesus: as His
    precious child.
Tell yourself that the purpose of your life is good. Imagine
    walking that out. How would that feel?
Give your life to Jesus. Trust Him with all of it.
Take time every day to pray and thank God for what He is
    going to do in your life.
Establish that as your identity.
Envision the future you've always wanted, without the
    negativity.

Jesus speaks God's Word to combat toxic thoughts, lies, and twisted truth.

Jesus was tempted in the wilderness by Satan. He had been fasting for forty days and was very hungry, so Satan tempted Him to turn the stones to bread. We, too, are often tempted to look for fulfillment in the things of this world or to manipulate our circumstances into what we want instead of trusting God's provision. But Jesus replied with the truth found in Scripture, "It is written: 'Man shall not live on bread alone, but on every word that comes from the mouth of God'" (Matthew 4:4).

Like Jesus, when we are tempted to believe lies or twisted truths, we need to remind ourselves of the truth from God's Word. It's life-bringing and sustaining to us. Proverbs speaks of the importance of following what God says rather than relying on our own wisdom: "Trust in the LORD with all your heart and lean not on your own understanding; in all your ways submit to him, and he will make your paths straight" (3:5-6).

Then Satan told Jesus to throw Himself off a cliff and command the angels to catch Him. Again, Jesus responded with scriptural truth: "It is also written: 'Do not put the Lord your God to the test'" (Matthew 4:7).

We are not meant to test God. He is the Almighty. Who better than Him to know what is best for us? We can instead say, "God's will be done." Our job is to obey and trust Him.

Satan next urged Jesus to worship him, promising that he would give Him the world.

Drawing on God's Word one more time, Jesus said to him, "Away from me, Satan! For it is written: 'Worship the Lord your God, and serve him only'" (Matthew 4:10).

When we bow to the things of this world we may get those things, but God says worship Him only, and that is what Jesus'

first reaction is throughout Scripture and
in this particular interaction with Satan:
He chooses to submit only to His Father.

*Seeking the fresh source of
the Word, the Holy Spirit,
and God's love will help us
combat the enemy.*

Note that when Jesus was tempted,
Satan actually used God's Word to try
to trap Him. That can happen to us too.
Truth twisted by religious oppression can make us feel trapped,
stagnant, and ashamed of who we are. Seeking the fresh source of
the Word, the Holy Spirit, and God's love will help us combat the
enemy's schemes.

PUT IT INTO PRACTICE:

Be prepared with Scripture verses that speak against the toxic
thoughts and lies that you tend to struggle with. (Review
the lists in chapter 7 for ideas.)

Remove any negative thoughts—any thoughts that hinder
the truth God speaks over your life.

Replace those negative thoughts with the truth from God's
Word.

Thank God for all of His good gifts and for His plans and
purpose for your future.

Jesus isn't moved by circumstances: He knows His priorities.

One day, as Jesus was out in a boat with His disciples, a storm broke
loose. The men were shaken and distressed, but how did Jesus react?

A furious squall came up, and the waves broke over the
boat, so that it was nearly swamped. Jesus was in the
stern, sleeping on a cushion. The disciples woke him and
said to him, "Teacher, don't you care if we drown?" He
got up, rebuked the wind and said to the waves, "Quiet!

Be still!" Then the wind died down and it was completely calm. He said to his disciples, "Why are you so afraid? Do you still have no faith?"

MARK 4:37-40

Jesus was unmoved by the storm, and He reminded His followers that if they have faith, they don't need to be rattled by difficult circumstances either. It is the same for us. When we remember who controls even the storms in our lives, we can set aside our fears and carry on with peace in our hearts. We can stay focused on our priorities instead of being distracted by our momentary troubles. Jesus didn't allow His life to be dictated by circumstances but was able to act with integrity in spite of them. You can do the same as you walk in truth and continually speak God's Word over your life.

Sometimes, others may have different expectations of what our priorities should look like. On another day, Jesus was going with Jairus, a synagogue leader, to heal his daughter who was ill. Along the way, a woman who had been sick for twelve years touched Jesus and was immediately healed. Jesus stopped to talk with her, saying, "Daughter, your faith has healed you. Go in peace and be freed from your suffering" (Mark 5:34). In other translations it says, "Your faith has made you whole."

Many would think Jesus shouldn't have let Himself be interrupted since He was already going to help Jairus's daughter. But Jesus stopped, and as we saw in chapter 6, He called this woman "daughter." He let His plans be shifted based on God's leading, despite what others may have thought. He stopped to love the ones in front of Him.

PUT IT INTO PRACTICE:
Do the most important things NOW! Don't wait. Allow God to lead you to what those most purposeful things are.

Do the things you are most scared of that are true to His Word, those things you push aside but know you need to do. Maybe it's breaking off a relationship. Maybe it's getting accountability for an addiction you've been struggling with. Love the ones God puts in front of you today. It might be scary, but you can do it.

Jesus creates proper boundaries to protect love.

The book of Mark tells us that "very early in the morning, while it was still dark, Jesus got up, left the house and went off to a solitary place, where he prayed" (1:35).

Jesus needed to spend time with His Father, and He practiced proper boundaries with others to ensure that could happen. Making space for God to speak is of the utmost importance for us, too, if we are to hear from Him and follow in His ways. Being in God's Word and having our hearts oriented around His truth is the foundation for our sense of worth. When we go to Jesus in those quiet places and ask Him to show us our position in Him, we aren't so easily compromised the rest of the day. Acting in the truth requires that we get our worth from God alone, allowing His Word to be our light and guide.

As we look at Jesus, we see a life of fulfillment and joy, and out of this grows the ability to bless others in love. As we spend time with God, we experience the depths of His love in a new and beautiful way, and we are able to pass that on to others.

PUT IT INTO PRACTICE:
Choose to thank God first thing in the morning.
Read God's Word each day before you look at your phone
    or eat.
Keep your phone out of your bedroom—or choose not to
    look at it until you're done reading God's Word.

Choose one verse that stands out to you from your morning
reading and repeat it throughout the day.

Take time each day and/or week to be away from distractions
and listen to God.

Keep a blessings journal or jar by your bed and thank God
for the beautiful things of the day each night.

Make time for a Christian retreat.

Claim the truth from God's Word about your identity. Don't
let others define you.

Place the truth of your identity in Christ on your mirror
or somewhere you will see it often. Speak the truth out
loud or in your head when you hear something that
contradicts it.

Stay away from anything that compromises your value
or worth. Place boundaries to keep out negative
influences.

Find ways to surround yourself with life-giving, positive
people and things.

Now that we have considered how to act in the truth, it's time
that we learn the secret weapon for combating the lies and breaking the cycles that have kept us down in our lives. Freedom is just
around the corner, and the truth will set you free to find healing
and experience wholehearted love.

MAKING IT PERSONAL

Scripture to Apply

Please take some time to read the Scriptures below. Take special
notice of calls to act in truth and of where your sense of true identity comes from. Summarize what you see in these verses in the
space provided below.

Then you will know the truth, and the truth will set you free. (John 8:32)

Dear children, let us not love with words or speech but with actions and in truth. (1 John 3:18)

Jesus answered, "I am the way and the truth and the life. No one comes to the Father except through me." (John 14:6)

We demolish arguments and every pretension that sets itself up against the knowledge of God, and we take captive every thought to make it obedient to Christ. (2 Corinthians 10:5)

Questions to Consider

1. What steps have you taken recently to take positive action based on truth?

2. In what other areas could you apply God's truth in the Bible to your life?

Call to Action

Think of a decision you recently had to make. Write down the thoughts and feelings you were experiencing. Then think about what God's Word has to say about the situation. How might your decision have been different based on this truth? Choose to take positive actions moving forward, surrounded by truth and empowered by the knowledge that God will give you the strength to conquer anything in your way.

The Freedom Cycle

SETTING YOURSELF UP
FOR THE LOVE YOU LONG FOR

CALEB'S STORY: FINALLY FREE

Something that I have hardly ever told anyone about is the sexual abuse that I experienced during my early adolescent years. It was a confusing and hurtful time that by the grace of God came to an end, but not without lasting effects that have trickled into my future.

It involved someone close to me, a relative (not in my immediate family) I looked up to at the time because of our shared interest in sports. What started with innocent hugging and touching turned into a full violation of my innocence and childhood. This person I trusted took advantage of me in every way. It opened doors to other sins that I had never pursued before that time. It continued for a few years until by God's grace, I found the courage to say *no*.

What followed was an addiction to pornography, a false sense of pleasure, and a lustful view of women, things I struggled with for many years. I often felt like a slave to my feelings, and my conscience would clang like an old church bell every time I turned to porn or looked at a woman lustfully. It left me feeling horrible and confused.

I had many "come to Jesus" moments in high school when I repented of my sin and determined to pursue God fully . . . only to falter again when I felt alone and lonely. It became increasingly harder to forgive myself. As I look back on those years, I thank God for a strong conscience that kept me from going further down the road of sin. It is His grace that saved me, again and again.

A few years after my biggest relationship breakup, I was finally able to fully break free of this addiction. I found myself lost again, watching shows and videos online that caused me to stumble, and never feeling the satisfaction or the love that I so desperately desired. I was always coming up empty and feeling awful about it.

One night, I decided that I'd had enough. I deleted all of my old bookmarks and erased my browsing history. I was going to live a pure lifestyle, one deserving of the love that I was seeking.

I stopped, stone-cold.

As I went to bed that night, feeling like an enormous weight was off of my shoulders, I began to hope again for the future—a future full of love and without the chains of addiction. A future in which I could share a life with someone who could see beyond my past and dream with me for things to come.

Even though the unhealthy behaviors had ended, I still needed to find healing in the aftermath. I had no idea of the long-term impact those years had had on me or of the destruction that followed. I needed to resolve the unforgiveness and pain I had been holding on to.

It wasn't until years later that Stefanie and I began to do the work of finding healing for those years of abuse in my life. One day, I decided to open up to her about my past. I had never told another soul about it my entire life. It was so hard. But as I talked, I could see her compassion and love as she cried over my pain.

Then we did something I had never done before: we applied the "freedom cycle" to my abuse and pain. She started with an exercise that walked me through my experience in a way that helped me to let Jesus reign over it fully. It enabled me to see that He was with me even in the moments of pain. She had me imagine the first time it happened, in a specific room in my relative's house. Then she had me picture Jesus entering the room, sitting beside me, never leaving. He was heartbroken over what was happening, and He was still there to hold me afterward. Each time after that, He was there too, never leaving me.

At first I had a hard time imagining how Jesus could be with me there, but as I brought the truth—Jesus—into the abuse, it brought me to a whole new level of healing and forgiveness. It allowed me to forgive my family member, taking control out of his hands and placing it into the hands of Jesus. Jesus could carry my pain; He could cover the sin committed against me. I didn't feel like I had to hide anymore. I could walk with freedom into my future, giving my past to Him.

PULLING IT ALL TOGETHER

We've spent a good deal of time with you, learning how to identify toxic thoughts, coping mechanisms, and toxic cycles. And we've seen how to recognize and act in the truth in each of these situations. But just knowing the truth doesn't always make it easy to act it out. The lies will still often feel more true in the moment than the truth. Staying connected to God can feel complicated and difficult (although He wants to make it easy).

Has God's amazing love and the true identity He's given you really sunk into your heart? Or are they easily brushed aside as you continue in all the old false narratives about yourself, others, and God? How do we get the truth of God to reach the places that need it the most so that we can find healing from past pain or trauma and experience wholehearted love as God intended?

This is where the *freedom cycle* comes in. The freedom cycle pulls together everything we have learned so that instead of continuing the negative or toxic cycle, we can insert the truth and overcome our usual unproductive responses. In this chapter, we will provide you with the tools you need to put the freedom cycle into play in your relationships. But let us start by giving you a quick example.

One day, I (Caleb) see an Instagram photo of someone on the beach who has six-pack abs and is sipping what looks like the best drink ever. It triggers the toxic thought in me, *I wish I could look like that, but I am not good enough.* This in turn might trigger me to eat something unhealthy to make myself feel better. Then I might gain weight and think *I'll never be good-looking enough.* And the cycle continues.

If instead I were to apply the freedom cycle, I would immediately tell myself the truth that I am beautifully and wonderfully created in the image of God. As I repeat that truth to myself, I believe it, and instead of acting out, I start a new and better pattern. I decide to mute that Instagram account, and then I do something I enjoy that feels purposeful: I write a post on "five truths about what God says about you." I feel like I am doing something meaningful and worthwhile by helping others believe the truth about themselves. Instead of going down a negative and toxic path, I am believing the truth about myself, and then living out the purpose that God created for me.

Walking with God's truth and His character will set you free. As

Scripture reminds us, when you stay connected to the Vine as the source of your strength, good things will flow from you and to you.

I am the true vine, and my Father is the gardener. He cuts off every branch in me that bears no fruit, while every branch that does bear fruit he prunes so that it will be even more fruitful. You are already clean because of the word I have spoken to you. Remain in me, as I also remain in you. No branch can bear fruit by itself; it must remain in the vine. Neither can you bear fruit unless you remain in me. I am the vine; you are the branches. If you remain in me and I in you, you will bear much fruit; apart from me you can do nothing.

JOHN 15:1-5

The battle over our hearts isn't one to take lightly, friend. Although your story might look very different from those in this book, you are still vulnerable to the same lies of the world that keep us separated from others. When we cope with our toxic thoughts through destructive sin patterns, it leads to so much heartbreak. It's in the humility of surrender to Jesus that we get to experience the truth of who we are and find full freedom.

WHERE WAS JESUS?

Where was Jesus in the midst of the relationship wounds you've received? You might not have been abused, but each of us believes toxic thoughts about ourselves, others, and God that have caused us to shut off part of our heart to the world. Like Caleb, you may have felt like God deserted you or that there's no way He could have been with you in your moments of deepest pain. But God wants to heal our childhood wounds.

Jesus hates all the suffering we've gone through, so much so that He came to be with us in the midst of it. Your pain has caused enough damage. The day has come to let Jesus' love enter the scene.

It's important to remember that Jesus isn't held to our version of time. Peter reminds us that "with the Lord a day is like a thousand years, and a thousand years are like a day" (2 Peter 3:8). It doesn't matter when our painful experiences happened. Jesus can heal memories from our past that are still hurting us in the present. As we bring Him these old wounds and memories, He wants to come in and help us find healing.

Think about your moment of greatest pain. What if you could have seen Jesus sitting with you, crying with you, and hurt by your pain? What if you could have heard God's voice saying, "This isn't a reflection of your value to Me. I sent My Son, Jesus, to die for you. You were worth it. I love you." Just think how different your view of yourself and of God might be.

Jesus hates the suffering we've gone through. He came to be with us in the midst of it.

How does this change the narrative of your life? As Caleb did, you can go back to those moments and picture the truth that He *was* with you and He never abandoned you. You can know that He was holding you even when you didn't know He was there. As you allow Jesus into your pain, He will cover over it with His love. This is a powerful exercise for finding healing for past pain. You can try this exercise on your own, or if you feel you need help and want to walk deeper into this type of healing, we recommend that you reach out to a Christian therapist. As you read on, we will give you more tools to help you find freedom over that pain from your past.

For current and ongoing issues, the freedom cycle helps you to believe God's truth over any toxic thought, and then act out of the fullness of God's love and truth. Each time you act in truth, it reinforces the truth of God over your life, which leads you to act in truth the next time you find yourself facing the same toxic thoughts. This cycle continues and grows stronger each time you put it into practice.

At the same time, we are able to help others break their toxic cycles because we can help them experience God's love in the midst of their pain, as our cycles intertwine. We can't control how they will receive the truth, but honoring others with our actions—as we act from a freedom cycle instead of a toxic cycle—can help set them up for success.[1]

TOOLS FOR THE FREEDOM CYCLE

One of the biggest blessings about owning a home now is that we have access to our own laundry equipment. We used to have to take our clothes to the end of the building, put in two dollars per load, and wait hours for it to finish. We are thankful not to have to deal with that anymore.

But one time, the dryer broke in the middle of January. When a dryer dies, it's terrible. You take out the clothes, expecting that warm, dry, and cozy feeling, but instead you have a cold, wet, and heavy mess. What the heck!

The repair company told us it would be two weeks before they could get out. TWO WEEKS? We sent some of our clothes back through the dryer, hoping the air would eventually dry them. Cycle after cycle, with the same results.

It wasn't until the repairman came, identified the problem, and replaced a part that the dryer began to work again. The same goes for toxic cycles. We have to identify the toxic thought and replace it with the truth to fix the cycle and walk forward in freedom.

It is vital to know how to get into the freedom cycle and how to get into it quickly. There are going to be triggers that try to push us back into that toxic cycle. But now we have the key to unlock us from the toxic prison. The freedom cycle gives us the knowledge and the tools we need.

First, as we've said before, we need to recognize when we are heading into a toxic cycle. There are two ways to do this:

1. *Identify that you are believing something untrue about yourself, others, or God.* If you are believing an untruth, when something bad happens, you act out in a destructive way.
2. *Recognize that you're coping in a way that is not good for you.* This might be overeating, oversleeping, diving deeper into addiction, or self-harm.

Those are two very clear indicators of being in a toxic cycle. At this point, you can put the freedom cycle into motion by asking yourself four questions that pull together everything we've been learning.

What am I feeling?

First, ask yourself, *What am I feeling?* There are different layers to what you feel in the moment you find yourself stuck in a toxic cycle. As we've learned, your heart rate will be going faster, you will feel the tension in your body, you may start getting a bad headache. You may feel anxious, overwhelmed, or stressed, or you may feel anger or unrest. These signals mean your triggers are being set off.

You may next start coping by yelling, withdrawing, or resorting to other unhealthy reactions. When you sense these responses, make a list in your head, write it down, or note it on your phone. *I'm feeling a lot of stress in my hands. I am feeling really anxious. I am feeling very angry.* Make sure to observe all the emotions you are experiencing. Don't worry about why you're feeling that way, just notice what you are feeling.

What am I believing?

The next step is to ask, *What am I believing?* and take note of your response. Again, don't worry about why you are believing it, just what you are believing in that moment.

It's important to identify the answers to these first two questions and write them down if you can. This way you have a template for your toxic cycle—what triggers you, what you are feeling, and what you are believing in those moments—which will be helpful in future situations.

What is the truth?

Once you've assessed the situation, ask yourself, *What is the truth?* The truth, as we've seen, is that you are loved, that you are beautifully and wonderfully made, that God has given you a purpose. Even if it doesn't feel that way right now, even if you've made a mistake, even if you don't feel worthy, the truth is that you are loved, you are not a mistake, and you have an amazing purpose.

How do I act when I believe the truth?

Now allow yourself to emotionally connect to that truth. Ask yourself, *How do I act when I believe the truth?*

When you believe that you are worthy and loved and that you have a purpose, you feel at peace and you can love yourself and others well. You are able to be kind, understanding, and forgiving to yourself and to others. It's powerful to believe the truth and then act in it in this way.

One of the most powerful things about this process is the understanding that you gain from seeing your thoughts and patterns in a clearer way. It helps you identify where you are getting stuck, how you feel when you get stuck, and then what you are believing about yourself, others, and God.

The freedom cycle takes practice, and you will get better at it the more you implement it. Please be gentle with yourself along the way. It becomes your thought process as you retrain your mind to switch from immediately believing toxic thoughts to now believing the truth and walking it out. It takes forty days to break a habit. Similarly, it will take time to re-see your pain, your triggers, your fears, and your anxiety from a new perspective. It will take commitment to replace the old patterns of behavior. But as Hargrave says, "Practicing the new thoughts and behaviors that run counter to the old executive operating system is absolutely essential if individuals are to learn new habits."[2] And we promise you, it is worth the effort. When we are purposeful about applying the freedom cycle, it is a game changer.

A REAL-WORLD EXAMPLE

Let's take a look at a practical example of how the freedom cycle works. Think about your marriage or your future marriage. One day your spouse is getting home from a long day of work, and you are excited to see them. You run outside to give them a hug, but they act very disinterested. Their reaction triggers you; you grew up with disinterested parents, and it developed the toxic thought in you that *I am unlovable.*

In the past, you would have gone off in this instance, yelling, blaming, and withdrawing because you felt unloved and rejected by your spouse. This would cause a massive argument and subsequent lonely evening for the both of you.

But at this moment, you are at a crossroads. You can go into your usual unhelpful coping behaviors, OR you can choose to activate the freedom cycle. Recognizing the signs of a toxic cycle, you ask yourself the four questions:

What am I feeling?
I am feeling anxious, frustrated, and rejected.

What am I believing?
I am believing that I am unlovable and that my husband is reject-ing me.

What is the truth?
The truth is that I am loved by my spouse, but they just finished a long, hard day at work. They didn't mean to hurt me; they are just tired.

How do I act when I believe the truth?
I choose to know I am loved in that moment, and I act in the truth by blessing my spouse in any way I can. Maybe I could bring in their bag or take their jacket at the door. Or I could say, "How can I support you in your stressful day?" or "Do you want to tell me about your day?"

Choosing to act in this way changes the tone of the whole interaction. Your spouse might then open up and say, "Well, my boss told me that I did a horrible job on that big project."

This might be a clue that your spouse is dealing with some toxic thoughts of their own. They may be feeling *I'm not good enough*. You might tell them you are so sorry that this person was mean and that you would love to know how you can make it better. You could order takeout and spend time listening to them talk about their day, or you could give them time to decompress so that they can be present with you later.

By acting in the truth you are best set up to be loved in your relationships, and so is the other person. They don't have to feel like they must always be on their best behavior; they know they will be appreciated either way. In turn, they will very likely love you better in the future, even when they've had a bad day, because of how you have treated them.

The freedom cycle is the gift that keeps on giving.

When the other person is triggered and lashing out at you, if you are able to act in your freedom cycle despite their behavior, it might even help them get out of their toxic cycle. People aren't always able to believe the truth in their moments of pain or when they are triggered. Sometimes they still get stuck in the toxic cycle. But when you act in the truth (instead of in a triggered state because of their response to you), there is a chance that they will receive your kindness and be shaken out of their usual pattern of behavior.

We hope you can see how powerful entering the freedom cycle can be. When you are emotionally connected to God's truth, it allows you to picture the outcome you hope for in the situation. It helps you picture the right behavior, or at least how it would feel to be appreciated, instead of your usual reaction. Maybe you picture your spouse or significant other giving you a hug and telling you how much they love you. These mental pictures can make a huge difference in retraining your mind. If you believe and know that your spouse is a great person and that they do love you, when they act out in a way that is not in line with their character, you won't immediately think they are a terrible person and get triggered. Instead, you can picture how well they treat you most of the time and then act from that mindset. If you are able to implement the freedom cycle in this way, the landscape of your relationship, especially in conflict, will change.

If you implement the freedom cycle, the landscape of your relationship will change.

Remember, no one will do this perfectly. You might mess up and act out sometimes, and you might handle it really well other times. People around you might mess up as well. Give yourself and others grace, knowing that relationships are complicated.

It all comes together when we ask those important questions any time we are triggered: *What am I feeling? What am I believing? What is the truth? How do I act when I know the truth?*

These questions allow you to do something different. They give you the choice and the chance to break the toxic cycle in your own life and in the lives of others you encounter. They do the same in those most important relationships—with yourself, with God, and with your spouse or love interest.

OTHER IMPORTANT CONSIDERATIONS

Let's take a look at a few other considerations for implementing the freedom cycle in our relationships. First, we need to keep in mind who the real enemy is. We also need to understand the importance of forgiveness for experiencing true freedom. Finally, we must maintain healthy boundaries.

Recognizing the Enemy

Have you ever seen a movie where the true bad guy wasn't revealed until the end? It always comes as a big surprise, the aha moment for the hero of the film. Recently, we were watching the TV series *The Book of Boba Fett*, about a famous Star Wars character trying to rebuild an empire after losing everything in the original movies.

When Boba Fett returns from a trip, he finds his family massacred, apparently killed in cold blood by a Star Wars version of a biker gang. He later gets revenge on the gang only to find out that it was actually a huge crime company that had done the deed. He had been fighting a false enemy, wasting his time, energy, and emotions.

In our lives it can feel the same. We experience pain, agony, and betrayal from those closest to us as they act out of the pain in their own lives. We think they are the enemy, so we choose to lash out against them, sometimes destroying relationships for good.

But our battle is not against them. The true enemy lurks in the dark, a big, bad thief who comes to steal, kill, and destroy. As the apostle Paul tells us, "Our struggle is not against flesh and blood, but against the rulers, against the authorities, against the powers of this dark world and against the spiritual forces of evil in the heavenly realms" (Ephesians 6:12).

Instead of feeling like your spouse, your boss, that person stuck in traffic with you, your neighbor, your sister, or your friend are the enemies, you will realize they aren't. When you are tempted to see things as a personal attack against you, take a step back again and realize it's their own sin, shame, and pain that is being triggered. Self-pity, self-focus, taking things too personally, overdramatic thinking, and playing the victim will be things of the past as you continue to walk into the freedom cycle and see others from the view of compassion instead of judgment.

As you realize that the people around you aren't your enemies, God isn't your enemy, and you aren't your own worst enemy, you will be able to fight the real enemy.

There is an enemy against your soul. Satan has been speaking lies from the beginning. He wants to pit husband against wife. Father against son. Friend against friend. As we see things from God's perspective, Satan will win fewer battles.

What if we stopped believing our love interest or spouse was the enemy? Or our parents or siblings, a friend or classmate, or our boss or coworker or a politician?

Penelope had a very angry dad. He yelled and said mean things when he was angry. Because of these experiences, she believed two narratives, both untrue but feeling very true to her: *My dad must be the worst dad in the world to hurt me in this way* and *I must be the worst little girl in the world.*

When Penelope believed *My dad must be the worst*, she found a way to escape. She started living in a fairy-tale world in her head, imagining a perfect family and a father who didn't hurt her. Penelope dreamed of being cherished, loved, and protected by her father.

When she thought *I must be the worst*, she started hurting herself. Anything that triggered her caused her to react in a way that resulted in physical or emotional harm to herself.

It wasn't until she stopped her black-and-white thinking that she found freedom.

During therapy, she talked through her father's life. He had a demanding, stressful job and had himself been abused in childhood. His rage disorder wasn't a reflection on the little girl, but of his own pain. As Penelope came to understand this, she was able to forgive her father. She started to see that she wasn't the worst little girl in the world. And she realized something else: she had been deeply believing that her father did not love her.

But her black-and-white thinking started becoming more colorful. She realized her dad's way of showing love was through acts of service and gifts. Her own love language was words of affirmation and quality time.[3] Her two biggest ways of receiving love were the ways that he hurt her the most, causing pain to her core.

The lack of love she felt from her father she also associated with God. For most people, how we experience our father's love, or lack thereof, is how we relate to God's love.

Penelope started to re-see herself and her dad. Her dad was working so hard to provide food, shelter, clothes, college, and so much more. He did love her. Realizing her dad wasn't her enemy was so powerful. Penelope started rethinking all those old painful memories from a different perspective.

Forgiveness and the Freedom Cycle

The freedom cycle is so important for forgiveness. Typically, when a person or couple is stuck in a toxic cycle, forgiveness becomes harder and harder the longer they are stuck.

In order to get the freedom you need, you must first forgive yourself and then forgive the person who wronged you. When you are walking in your freedom cycle, you are more able and willing to forgive the other person because you know the truth about them. Knowing the truth doesn't mean they can't still hurt you. It just means that you know their true character, which leaves space for them to own up to what they have done. When you give grace to yourself and extend it to others, it brings a new level of freedom and intimacy that every relationship needs.

Often, when people are stuck in their toxic cycles, they spend a ton of time dealing with the coping mechanism, rather than the core issue. For example, when you get into a toxic cycle in a relationship, you may say something that hurts the other person. Much of the time, your saying something hurtful is not the real issue. It's only the way you *cope* with the real issue, which is a core toxic thought that has been triggered.

When you are able to first take responsibility for your words or actions, and then ask probing questions about what the other person is feeling, or why your comments hurt them so badly, you can get past the surface and into the deeper healing that needs to happen. You'll be able to get to the heart of the problem faster and find forgiveness.

Boundaries and the Freedom Cycle

There is often confusion around forgiveness and boundaries. People say, "You are a Christian. You are supposed to forgive everything." It is true that we are told to forgive seventy times seven (see Matthew 18:22) and to forgive just as God forgave us (see Ephesians 4:32). However, there is a difference between forgiving others and allowing their behavior to continue hurting you. It's okay to not have them in your life anymore—or at least to no longer allow certain parts of their behavior to impact you.

This is not an excuse to get out of marriage or to fire a subordinate at work. Rather, it's a way to protect yourself from a behavior that takes you outside of your integrity.

Dr. Henry Cloud says in his book *Changes That Heal*, "Many times people do sin against us when exercising their freedom, and we are responsible for dealing with the injury. If we don't, we will stay stuck in a blame position, powerless against their sin. This 'victim' mentality keeps many people stuck in their pain."[4]

You don't have to take responsibility for the wrongs done to you. You had no control over them. But taking responsibility for what you can do in response is the key to moving forward in freedom.

Setting boundaries around things that steal our love is helpful. We think often about how Jesus sent out His disciples. He told them, "If anyone will not welcome you or listen to your words, leave that home or town and shake the dust off your feet" (Matthew 10:14). Jesus set boundaries for them, knowing that not everyone would accept their teaching. We follow a Savior who ultimately was killed by those who opposed Him. As we walk in His footsteps, we will also face opposition.

Note too that there is a difference between forgiveness and reconciliation.

Forgiveness: no longer holding anger or resentment over an offense or mistake someone has committed
Reconciliation: restoring a relationship to a friendly status

We forgive out of our obedience and love for God, but God doesn't call us to stay in a close relationship with everyone. Jeremiah 29:11 makes clear the type of life God intends for us to have: He has "plans to prosper you and not to harm you, plans to give you hope and a future."

If you are in harm's way, it's actually more loving to protect yourself and others from that harm. It's also loving to the hurtful person, because unless they realize their actions have consequences, they will continue in that behavior. As we leave room for them to experience the natural consequences of their behavior, they will have to face the truth or they will be judged by God.

Seeing changed behavior over time is how you can tell if reconciliation can be part of your story with the person who has harmed you. Not every person is meant for us in every season of life. But every person is meant to be forgiven.

Walking into freedom isn't always simple. There are many factors to consider and so many triggers and events in everyday life that can derail you. But God's purpose for your life is so amazing. Our prayer is that you can claim it each day by choosing to use the freedom cycle over your toxic thoughts.

STEFANIE'S STORY: MIXED SIGNALS

Caleb and I have toxic thoughts that can really play uniquely together in mutually assured destruction. But as we continue to claim the truth about each other, we are able to stop the toxic cycles that want to form in our marriage.

Caleb grew up the middle child. He was the loudest out of his brothers and the most outgoing. His brothers played off this fact, so Caleb would be the one most likely to get in trouble. Even if he wasn't a part of the mayhem, his brothers knew how to push his buttons to make it seem like it was his fault. As a result, Caleb formed the toxic thought *Everyone is out to get me and blame me.*

He coped by trying with all his might to do everything right. He hated conflict and getting in trouble. Sitting in his room reading for his time-out while his brothers played outside his window broke his little spirit. *If I'm just better, I won't get in trouble like this again*, he thought.

As a highly sensitive little girl, I had the biggest desire for words of affirmation and for quality time with the ones I loved. I longed to play with my mom and dad. But they were both busy doing things for my sister and me. My parents are both people of few words when it comes to compliments and affirmation. I would ask them, "Do you like my drawing? Am I pretty? Do you love me?"

Each time I asked them to play with me, each time I hinted for a compliment and was met with resistance, I was crushed. I began to believe the toxic thoughts *I am unlovable* and *No one wants to be around me*. I compensated by trying to evoke responses (any kind of attention was better than less attention) and to show I was fun to hang out with. But if I saw even the slightest hint of resistance to playing with me, or if someone was not excited to give me a positive comment, it would reinforce the lies.

Here I am with my toxic thoughts of *I am unlovable* and *No one wants to be around me*. And here Caleb is with his toxic thoughts of *Everyone is out to get me and blame me*.

As you might expect, a cycle has occurred many times in our marriage based on these toxic thoughts colliding.

It's a Saturday. A day Caleb and I usually hang out together. I wake up with full energy and excitement to spend time with the love of my life. I ask him early in the morning, "Do you want to go on a hike with me right now?"

Caleb gives a little grunt and turns over on his side. We both fall back asleep, but my little toxic thought is screaming in the back of my mind.

When we wake up, Caleb works hard to be good and show me he loves me. He makes me breakfast, fixes hot chocolate, empties the dishwasher, and puts in a load of laundry. I mention several things we could do that sound fun to me. "Hey Caleb, would you like to go to the mall, or go hiking, or go golfing with me today?"

My tone doesn't give away excitement about one particular thing. I'm not letting him know what I want to do, because I'm scared of rejection. With no excitement in his own voice, he responds, "I don't care, what do *you* want to do?"

There it is. My toxic thought screams back at me, *See, no one is excited to hang out with me. He doesn't want to have fun with me.*

"Thanks for the breakfast and for doing the laundry," I tell him as I yawn.

"Are you tired?"

"Yes, I am!" My toxic thoughts have been harassing me since this morning. They've exhausted me even though I've been unaware of what's been happening.

"Why don't you just relax on the couch, and I'll take care of anything that would bless you today," says Caleb. He folds the laundry, does some yard work, and cleans the house. I sit on the couch alone, thinking that Caleb doesn't like spending time with me. The toxic cycle is bubbling over.

When he comes in from hours of work, I start yelling at him.

"You don't care about me. You never want to spend time with me. You don't like to have fun with me!" I start sobbing, and I run into our bedroom, slamming the door.

Caleb is shocked. He's been working hard all day to show how much he cares about me. And here I am telling him the opposite. His toxic thoughts are triggered big time. *Everyone is out to get me and blame me* seems to be his life story and one that he can't escape from. Caleb tries to calm me down, but as I continue yelling, he gets defensive.

"I've worked so hard for you all day," Caleb says in an angry tone. "I do everything for you. How can you be so crazy?"

And *my* toxic thought is triggered again. *See, he doesn't like to be around me because he thinks I'm crazy.* This toxic conflict cycle continues for hours, and we get so discouraged. We both are trying so hard, we love each other so much, yet we feel discouraged, unloved, and unappreciated.

Thankfully, once Caleb and I became intentional about learning each other's toxic cycles—what was going on beneath the surface—we were able to totally change this narrative we were stuck in.

Now we both are able to set each other up for success. Caleb knows my desire for fun with him, and I'm more direct in my communication and let him know the day before if I desire to do something fun so we can plan accordingly. He is adamant about telling me how much he loves hanging out with me. That there is no one in the world he enjoys spending time with more than me. That I'm the most fun person in the world to him. This speaks directly against my toxic thoughts and has helped me feel safe to tell him when I want to spend time with him.

> *As we are filled with God's truth over toxic thoughts, we can show others God's love.*

I'm now able to give Caleb more grace when I feel misunderstood. I start conversations more gently, telling Caleb how much I appreciate him for the little and big things I see him do. If I need to bring up something that could be interpreted as "wrong" or "bad," I'm careful with how I word it so I don't trigger his toxic thoughts.

When one of us ends up upset in a toxic thought, the other is usually able to speak the truth in the moment and stop the toxic cycle. We are able to enter into the freedom cycle more quickly, more easily, and more naturally. It doesn't mean that we've never faced a toxic cycle again, but they are shorter, and the conflict is much more quickly resolved because we see who the real enemy is. We help comfort each other in our pain and have become a safe place for each other as we've built trust over time.

Dr. Martin Luther King Jr. says it well: "Darkness cannot drive out darkness; only light can do that. Hate cannot drive out hate; only love can do that."[5]

As we are filled with God's truth over our toxic thoughts, we are able to show others God's love (even when they aren't showing love back to us). As we are connected to the true Vine of love, all His goodness can flow through us onto others. We don't need them to give out something to us. We are already getting what we need from a source that others can't see.

We can complicate God's love. But it's really the most simple and beautiful love story ever told. And it's our story. Jesus loves us beyond measure. There's nothing that can separate us from His love. He's forgiven us as far as the east is from the west. Walking out this life with our unshakable identity as His children is so freeing. As we experience the love of Christ, our natural response is to live and walk in His ways. As we follow Him and are obedient to His words, it keeps setting us up to live loved and to give love.

MAKING IT PERSONAL

Scripture to Apply

We invite you to read the Scriptures below. Notice where your strength comes from and the hope that God speaks over your life. Summarize what you see in these verses in the space provided below.

> He said to me, "My grace is sufficient for you, for my power is made perfect in weakness." Therefore I will boast all the more gladly of my weaknesses, so that the power of Christ may rest upon me. For the sake of Christ, then, I am content with weaknesses, insults, hardships, persecutions, and calamities. For when I am weak, then I am strong. (2 Corinthians 12:9-10, ESV)

If we confess our sins, he is faithful and just to forgive
us our sins and to cleanse us from all unrighteousness.
(1 John 1:9)

"I know the plans I have for you," declares the LORD,
"plans to prosper you and not to harm you, plans to give
you hope and a future." (Jeremiah 29:11)

You are a chosen people, a royal priesthood, a holy
nation, God's special possession, that you may declare the
praises of him who called you out of darkness into his
wonderful light. (1 Peter 2:9)

Do not forget this one thing, dear friends: With the Lord
a day is like a thousand years, and a thousand years are
like a day. (2 Peter 3:8)

God is love, and all who live in love live in God, and God
lives in them. (1 John 4:16, NLT)

Questions to Consider

1. Think about a painful moment in your past. How would it
    change your perspective on that experience to picture Jesus
    being beside you in your pain?

2. What is something you enjoy doing that gives you a sense of purpose? How could you incorporate that into your own freedom cycle?

3. Who have you been seeing as the enemy in your own toxic cycles? How would you see those cycles differently if you recognized the true enemy?

4. Is there someone in your life who you have found it hard to forgive? What steps could you take to begin moving toward forgiveness?

Call to Action

Think of a toxic thought you are believing or a past pain you have experienced. Speak the truth from the Bible directly against that toxic thought and believe the truth. Allow Jesus to cover that past pain or core toxic thought you believe. Let the truth dictate your actions. Begin a new cycle—a cycle of truth over toxic thought. Do something purposeful, something that makes you feel the truth about yourself and about the way that God made you uniquely and purposefully in your mother's womb. Repeat the truth. Continually speak it over yourself and over the toxic thoughts and past pain that you have experienced.

10

Seen, Known, Loved

CLAIMING YOUR NEW STORY
IN THE LIGHT OF GOD'S LOVE

CALEB'S STORY: FULLY ALIVE

"Tag, you're it!"

Stefanie slapped my shoulder and took off running across the lawn at Art Hill in Forest Park, in St. Louis, Missouri.

As she ran through the grass, the cool air blowing gracefully through her hair, she seemed to float like an angel. The sky was full of bright pink and orange tones, like a freshly painted canvas, a masterpiece only the Louvre would own. The sunset was a perfect backdrop for our romantic evening. Stefanie had the biggest smile on her face—the kind you get when you've found a childhood treasure you lost long ago. She soared up the hill, full of joy.

I couldn't take my eyes off of her. Tears began to stream down my face as I saw my bride living fully alive, the way God made her to be. With each step, another weight seemed to fly off her shoulders, shattering on the ground in the wake of God's amazing grace. I'm sure she broke world records as she ran up that hillside. I had never seen her so free.

Those few seconds felt like a lifetime as I allowed each one to be etched on my heart like a metalsmith engraving a plaque. The beauty of the moment was too much to take in, as if every epic love song were playing at once, a symphony of the fullness of love.

Finally remembering that I was "it," I ran after her, and she had never been so hard to catch. I eventually wrapped her in my arms, swung her around, and tagged her back. We danced and played for an hour, running up and down the hill, ear-to-ear smiles on our faces. The people around us must have thought we had lost it, but quite the contrary: I felt like we had found it—a piece of heaven.

I never wanted it to end. But as the sun began to set, we walked back to our car. We took in the view, hand in hand, not wasting a second as we took note of every beautiful thing about each other and the scene around us. This was far better than any movie could have depicted, and in those moments, I never felt more loved by Stefanie, or by God.

It's moments like these that make all the mess I've experienced in this life worth it.

This is wholehearted love.

BETTER THAN THE MOVIES

We have come a long way together in this book. We hope that you are already starting to see how the ideas we've covered could change your approach to life in general and relationships in particular. As you continue identifying those toxic thoughts, coping mechanisms, and toxic cycles that have kept you from the future you dream of, we pray you will begin to act in the truth more and more and that you will learn to trust God with the details. Little by little, you will find healing from past pain or trauma and be ready to experience wholehearted love as God intended.

We have always been fans of love. We have several favorite romantic movies and TV shows, as we're sure you've noticed! There is something captivating about how people fall in love. For us, it is encouraging to see how others have found the love the two of us share—and not just in the movies, but in real life too. We hope and pray that our friends and acquaintances can keep their love alive.

We've heard time and time again that true love is not like they show it in the movies. Genuine romance takes hard work, trust, and sacrifice over time, they say. That's where you will experience love. Does hard work and sacrifice sound appealing? If you're being honest, probably not.

We want to propose a different way of looking at wholehearted love: it is *better* than the movies. Experiencing this wholehearted love requires two things. First, wholehearted love must be intentional, and second, it must have God at its core. Intentional love in a relationship, coupled with intentional love for God, produces love that is unconditional and wholehearted, a love in which we feel fully seen and known.

Wholehearted love must be intentional.

Wholehearted love requires that you be intentional, from the beginning, about nurturing and supporting your partner. This means that you go about your day intentionally finding ways to express your love for them. Some might call this sacrificial or hard work love, but however you choose to label it, it simply means being deliberate or purposeful in your words and actions.

If you find the love of your life, your purpose in the relationship should be to love them every single day, in the best way you know how. If you don't know how, you learn how. You purposefully take care of them, in sickness and health, as long as you live.

When you operate this way from the beginning, it sets you up for long-term success. It ensures that ten years down the road you will still experience the butterflies—you know, the kind you feel when your partner first touches your hand and you are sure you could fly to the moon.

Just because it feels amazing doesn't mean that everything will go perfectly. You still need to be intentional and alert, seek out mentors, and find support from people in your community and/or from a trusted professional as you walk in this journey. The enemy is always lurking around the corner, and he takes any opportunity to put a wedge in your relationship, causing your toxic cycle to start over again and collide with your partner's.

Wholehearted love is better than the movies. Why? Because when you walk into a relationship with your whole heart, choosing intentionality from the beginning—daily determining to believe God's truth over toxic thoughts and to implement the freedom cycle— you are choosing a deeper connection than the movies will ever be able to show you.

Wholehearted love must have God at its core.

The other, and most essential, part for a wholehearted love that is better than the movies is having God at your core. Whether you are involved with someone or not, a close relationship with God is so much better than any other kind of love.

God loves far more deeply than any person ever could. His love is the kind that parts a sea so people can walk through it to safety, the kind that heals people from lifelong illness. It's the kind that sends His only Son to die for you and for us.

One of our favorite worship songs is "Reckless Love" by Cory Asbury, which showcases the amazing, inspiring love of God, describing it as reckless in a way. But God's love for you is far more than just being reckless. His love is the fullest pursuit of you. There is nothing He wouldn't overcome to capture your heart.

The best part is that God will never let you down. He is the ever-present, awe-inspiring God of the universe. He's like a great, conquering explorer, crossing the roughest seas, climbing the highest snowcapped peaks, and walking through the hottest fiery coals just to save you from your battles and bring you back to life.

As you have seen through our stories, it isn't God who lets us down in our painful moments, but rather our perception of Him through the lens of our toxic thoughts. He never changes. He was always there in our painful moments, seeking to woo us back to Himself.

He wants a close relationship with you too. Draw close to Him, and He will draw close to you (see James 4:8). Wholehearted love starts with God. He wants you to know His love for you, and He's waiting for you to choose to love Him back. No relationship could ever be better than a close, intimate relationship with God, through Jesus.

Friend, you can have a love far greater than the movies.

The two of us feel more in love with each other now than we did the day we started dating. We still act like those young lovebirds, laughing, flirting, and going on adventures together even ten years later. It doesn't get old. It gets better.

What's the secret?

Love God more than your spouse. Love your spouse more than yourself. And intentionally love both of them each day, from the start of the relationship.

Well, what if you've been married for forty years and are tired of each other?

There is never a better day than today to start intentionally loving God with your whole heart, and learning to love and forgive yourself too. Then, out of the love you have for God, you can start loving your spouse intentionally with your whole heart.

Wholehearted love isn't like the movies. It is so much better.

LEARNING TO LOOSEN YOUR GRIP

Sometimes we have to give up control of the thing that we want the most so that we will be able to fully enjoy it some day in the future. When we seek to control circumstances around us and have too firm of a grip on them, we don't leave room for God to work.

Think about raccoons. (Yes, raccoons.) They love shiny objects. When they find one, they tend to hold on to it and not let go. A raccoon will reach inside a trap to grab hold of a gleaming item, but then its paw is too large to get back out of the trap. The raccoon can let go of the object and remove its paw, or it can hold on and be caught. Raccoons invariably choose to keep their grasp on the item, thus sealing their fate.

If we are not careful, we will fall into the same trap. We may be mesmerized by every new idea that is hyped as the answer to all of our troubles. We may be drawn to the shiny, new object instead of letting God fulfill His plan for our lives.

For me (Caleb), loosening my grip meant giving up control of the thing I wanted most: a wife. I had spent years holding on to the thought that I needed someone in my life, and it seemed the only way to make that happen was through my own efforts. Can you blame me? I had been living my life for God, only to have my dream come crashing down. The pain of the past caused me to take too much control over my future. But I finally let go, which allowed God to do a work in me during that time in between.

And He worked out the details so much better than I ever could have. Stefanie is far better than any list of attributes I could have imagined in a life partner. If I had gone after someone who fit my own list, I might never have found the love of my life.

Being open to what God has for us allows us to fully enjoy the middle parts of our lives. I frequently tell people that the "waiting season," while difficult, is one of the best times for growth and maturity both in our relationship with God and in our character. It allows us to focus on areas that need improvement and ways that we can grow closer to God. We can become financially viable not only for our own security but also so we're prepared to take care of a future partner, and we can become physically healthy not only for our own well-being but also in order to live longer with our spouse. There are so many ways that we can better ourselves in those seasons in order to be ready should God bring someone into our lives.

> *Being open to what God has for us allows us to fully enjoy the "waiting season."*

What are the "shiny objects" that are holding your attention and making it difficult for you to let go? Are you ready to give them up and trust God with the details of your love life?

WHERE TO FOCUS YOUR THOUGHTS

When you have decided to give God control of your life and you are now in a waiting season, it is important to know where to focus your mind. In what areas does God want you to grow and improve? The book of Philippians offers some good guidance: "whatever is true, whatever is noble, whatever is right, whatever is pure, whatever is lovely, whatever is admirable—if anything is excellent or praiseworthy—think about such things" (4:8).

Focusing on these qualities allows our minds and hearts to be more aligned with what God values. By the way, these are also excellent traits to look for in a future mate, and if you are already married, they can have a great impact on your marriage as well.

You see what you want to see unless you focus your eyes on the things that are important to God. Let's break down this list of qualities a little further.

Whatever Is True

Have you ever played the game two truths and a lie? How it works is that one person states three things about themselves, two of which are true, and one of which is a lie. It is up to the other players to decide which statement is untrue.

Obviously, the better you know a person, the easier it is to recognize the lie. You can surely guess that when the two of us play together, it's easy for us to detect each other's lies.

It seems significant that "whatever is true" is listed first out of all these traits we are told to focus on. As we fix our thoughts on the truth about God and ourselves, it allows us to operate in our fullest self and with the truest of motives.

It works like this. When I (Caleb) met with my counselor who advised me that I was not good enough to play college basketball, I had two choices. I could believe the truth about myself, which was that I *was* good enough, or I could believe the lie that I wasn't. In this case, I believed the truth, and I was able to operate fully in the knowledge that if I worked hard enough, I would be able to play at the level I wanted to. If I had believed the lie, or toxic thought, about myself, I would never have made it.

The enemy speaks lies and toxic thoughts over us daily to keep us from focusing on what is true. God calls us to live in the truth of who He says we are so that we can live out of the fullness of His love for us.

Whatever Is Noble

Noble means "having or showing fine personal qualities or high moral principles and ideals."[1] As we focus our minds on what is noble, we will notice those things that have meaning and honorable characteristics. This causes a powerful shift in our mindset, and we begin to see those exact qualities in others.

For example, one of our favorite practices each day is to name one to three things that we are thankful for. Not only does it remind us of the goodness of God but it trains us to think of thankfulness before anything else. That way, when bad days come along (which they will), we can easily shift our thoughts away from the negative to the good and important things going on in our lives.

Being thankful also allows us to see thankfulness in others. It makes itself known in the attitude and mindset of those who practice it despite their circumstances. As you go on dates, you can identify the noble qualities about the other person, making it easier to know if the two of you might be a good match. Or as you notice those qualities in your spouse, it will strengthen your love for them.

Whatever Is Right

Living in a way that is right depends on your definition of the truth and on what you believe. If you believe that God lays out right and wrong in the Bible, you have a good understanding of how to focus your mind on what is right.

The dictionary definition of right is "morally good, justified, or acceptable."² As people who love Jesus, we have to understand that what is good, justified, or acceptable in the world's eyes is completely different from what the Bible says. A normal or societal understanding of right versus wrong is not going to get you to the place God wants you to be, according to Philippians. What you need instead is an understanding of the heart of Jesus.

Jesus says that the two greatest commandments are to love the Lord our God with all our heart, mind, soul, and strength, and to love others as ourselves (see Matthew 22:36-40). This is what is right and good. And as you walk into a relationship, you learn to love others as you would yourself. In a marriage, as you wake up each day, loving God first, and then your husband or wife as you would yourself, it changes how you look at them, and how you look at yourself.

As we follow what is right, God allows us to become righteous before Him. This unlocks the freedom of His grace in our lives, and we can discern the right person and the right attitude for moving forward.

Whatever Is Pure

Purity can have several different connotations, but most people think in terms of sexual purity, specifically before marriage. The Bible is very clear about what is best. However, over time, people (specifically Christians) have confused human self-righteousness for God's design.

Purity culture has rampaged through the church over the years. What started out as a way to honor God through abstaining from sexual activity until marriage turned into a movement of shaming and ridiculing sexual behavior and alienating talk of such a nature in Christian circles. This caused confusion and pain for many living under such strict and hurtful ideologies, especially women.

We believe that purity in regard to sexual things is good. And specifically, it is best (according to God's Word) that we not have sex until marriage. Sex is a beautiful thing and is best enjoyed in the context of marriage. This is the way that God intended for it to be experienced. But just because someone has not followed through with this in the past, doesn't mean they are "unpure" forever. Purity is something that can be gained. Each time we seek God, our heart and mind become more pure. He makes us a new creation and wipes away the old!

Waiting until marriage is amazing, but when it is idolized (like anything else in life), it can become a hindrance and a stumbling block. Pornography addictions run rampant in church circles for both men and women, but especially for men. Purity stands in contrast to the teachings of mainstream culture, which says do what's best for you and do whatever you feel like doing. And they say that anyone who tells you otherwise is being judgmental.

Having age appropriate, real conversations in the church about these topics without shame can be so healing. Sex is beautiful and wonderful. It was designed by God for the context of marriage.

Shaming people's bodies, or sex in general, has hurt many in the church. Having a safe place to talk about desires and how to stay pure in your heart and mind with accountability is key. But we can only be accountable when we feel safe to share openly and honestly.

In this confusion about purity, people who love Jesus and the church need to stand as a beacon of hope for those who feel lost in a sea of doing what feels good. To be pure, by definition, is to not be contaminated by any other substance. When the Bible calls us to be pure, it is speaking to what Romans 12 tells us: "Do not conform to the pattern of this world, but be transformed by the renewing of your mind. Then you will be able to test and approve what God's will is—his good, pleasing and perfect will" (verse 2).

Being pure means not conforming to the world, not letting the world contaminate or adulterate our mind, soul, or heart. Instead, we are to be tethered to the truth of God and walking it out daily. Purity is not simply about perfect behavior versus promiscuity. It is about being close to God, fixing our eyes and heart on Him,

> *Be tethered to the truth of God and walk it out daily.*

letting go of the desires and temptations of this world, and only letting in what is best for us. And that is Jesus.

Trust your gut. When you think something might take you outside of your integrity, don't do it. Often, God gives us signs throughout our day—you might think of it as your conscience—and we don't listen. We need to listen to the Holy Spirit's prompting and act on it. When we do, God will direct us down the path that we should go. Purity isn't a set of rules, it's a way of focusing our eyes and heart on Jesus and forgoing anything that will take us away from Him.

Whatever Is Lovely

In a minute, we are going to ask you to close your eyes. Before you do, begin to think about something that you absolutely delight in. Whether it's that cozy, warm cup of coffee in the morning that helps you ease into the day, or maybe something beautiful that takes your breath away, try to remember how it makes you feel.

Now close your eyes and take note of the thoughts, feelings, and sensations connected to that delightful experience.

For you this might be a favorite childhood memory or possibly the day you got a promotion. For me (Caleb), it was that moment at Forest Park. It's a huge park and it all seems to roll on as far as the eye can see. Romance seemed to swirl around us like a cool breeze, and Stefanie's tagging touch was like a lightning bolt through my body. I stood there mesmerized by the sight of her running as fast as she could go. I often think of this moment on a hard day. It was a moment of delighting in the wife of my youth. She was lovely.

There are so many of these moments that we quickly brush by. If we would only stop and take them in, studying what is lovely all around us, what a difference it could make in our day. Having a moment to delight in helps us to remember what it's like to live fully alive.

Fixing our eyes on what is lovely reminds us that life is more than a nine-to-five job or a Netflix series we binge-watch. It is best lived in the small moments that God speaks to us through our experiences. Look for the lovely and delight in the little things, and it will open your heart to the beautiful ways that God loves on you. Looking for the lovely in life might even lead you right to the person that God has waiting for you.

Whatever Is Admirable

"That's very admirable" is a phrase we use when we see someone acting in a way that shows unexpected honor or respect toward someone else. Sometimes in our culture it has a connotation almost of being a joke. For example, when a woman makes it clear in the middle of a first date that she is not interested in pursuing a relationship, the guy may respectfully understand and buy dinner anyway. His friends might say, "That was admirable of you after she just rejected you."

Such sentiments are rampant in our society. When people do the "right thing" even when they are in a losing situation, they are called admirable. When you are acting admirably, it is nothing to be ashamed of. It is doing the right thing no matter what the outcome is. It's being respectful even if you are not being treated that way in return, it's doing something nice when it's unexpected, it's serving others even if you are supposed to be served. Sound like someone you know? This is exactly the life Jesus modeled for us.

When you act admirably, doing the unexpected, it makes you more like Jesus, and when you are more like Jesus, you live a fuller, happier, and more fulfilling life.

The next time you have a choice, choose what is admirable, and you will bring honor to others and help people to see Jesus. In addition, you will attract people to yourself who also follow Jesus.

Whatever Is Excellent or Praiseworthy

What is the most excellent thing that you have ever seen? What made it excellent? Was it the way it was done or how it was made? Or maybe it was the majesty of creation? What was excellent about what you saw?

For me (Caleb), the way Michael Jordan played basketball was excellent. Everything he did on the court was majestic and almost perfect. Every move was like a symphony as he dominated the court to the tune of six championships and several individual accolades. That's why many consider him "the GOAT" (the greatest of all time).

Sometimes people even hold him up as the example of excellence for another sport. They say, "He's the Michael Jordan of tennis" or "She's the Michael Jordan of women's soccer." When I want to set my mind on excellence, I think about how I can be like Michael Jordan. I ask myself, "Is what I am doing praiseworthy?"

When we think of excellence, our minds should focus on what is outstanding and extremely good. As you develop standards for yourself and for evaluating a potential mate, focusing on what is excellent or praiseworthy is a good guide.

Each person is uniquely gifted and talented at specific tasks. We become excellent at skills we have worked on our whole lives. Understanding this helps us to not only appreciate how God has gifted us but to see the ways that others exhibit excellence. It helps us narrow down the types of excellence we might require of people we want to be in a relationship with.

BELIEVING THE TRUTH ABOUT YOURSELF

The list of qualities in Philippians is a great place to start as you move toward healing from past pain and wait for God to bring wholehearted love into your life. But as our journey together draws to a close, we want to remind you again of a truth we've stated repeatedly in this book: God has made you uniquely and for a great purpose.

When we were in school, we always thought the most valuable people were the ones who were really good at math, reading, or sports, or who always got the best grades. But we started to realize that someone who was really great at writing might be terrible at swimming, or they might get along well socially but have a hard time with math.

We hope you're able to receive the great worth that God places on your life. This is countercultural because our society values people by what they can do for the world. The more talented someone is, the more special they are. The more money they make, the more highly we regard them.

Singers such as Selena Gomez are seen as more valuable because of the number of hits they come out with, the amount of money they make, or their follower count on Instagram. This is a lie that holds so many people back. If you were to meet Selena Gomez, you might be starstruck, as if she were superhuman and so much better than every other person. But if we pull back the curtain, we see that she is neither superior nor inferior to any of us. Instead, she is beautifully and wonderfully created by God, just like us.

On the other hand, people can experience the opposite end of the spectrum. They may struggle with addiction or mental illness, or they may have been through extremely hard times or have come from a difficult family situation. Some people might feel superior to them, but the truth is that God values them just the same.

We used to go to a church in downtown Los Angeles—Echo Park to be exact. The church feeds about fifty thousand people a month, and they house hundreds of people. The church has many programs that bring full restoration to people's lives, ridding them of addiction and past pain, and giving them a chance to dream again. It is such a special place to us.

The more we got to know the people going through the church's programs, the more they became our heroes. They have so much courage, and we appreciate the way they respect others, their gratefulness for a second chance, and their beautiful stories of God's redemption. Believing the truth that they are valuable to God helps them get back on their feet and get their lives together.

As you apply the new truths you have learned throughout this book, you are our hero too! It does take courage to begin changing old ways of coping with pain. But you are worth the effort. Think about the lists of truths from God's Word that we considered in chapter 7. Remind yourself of how God views you and of your value in Him. The truth is that your value is not dictated by your circumstances. It's dictated by your Creator, and He made you beautifully and wonderfully!

CLAIMING YOUR NEW STORY

Dear friend, are you ready to claim your new story in light of God's bigger story? Are you ready to exchange any toxic thought, continually and consistently, for God's truth? Are you ready to fight the right battles with the armor of God? Remember that you are not alone. You are loved beyond measure, and God does have a beautiful purpose for your life. You are part of the greatest love story ever told. You are loved by the King of the universe. He wants to know you. He sees you. He loves you more than you can fathom.

Imagine meeting the King of kings today. You might hear Him address you by name and share these words with you:

Dear one, I know it's been so difficult for so long. I know you think these masks and the ways you've coped have been protecting you. Your heart has been torn apart, and you needed a way to hold it together. You thought you had found some ways, but they've been doing you more harm than good. What if there was a different way? Better armor? A chance to resolve your fears and be healed to your core?

I am the King of kings and Lord of lords. I'm the Alpha and the Omega—the beginning and the end. And I want to help you.

Imagine Jesus taking you in His arms. He knows everything you've ever done, and He isn't weighed down by your shame, regret, or pain. Everything hidden is now exposed, but you feel no shame. He wipes you clean.

Hear Him say to you, "My child, be well."

Feel Him making you brand new today. Feel the freedom of being loved to your core. Hear Him tell you, "I have new armor for you."

Take His sword, helmet, boots, belt, breastplate, and shield (see Ephesians 6:10-17).

This is the armor of My Father. As you put these on each day, you won't need to fear. You will have everything you need to fight the battles that come your way and to know the right battles to fight. Remember that you'll never do it alone.

The secret to living life wholeheartedly is understanding the truth about who you are and who created you. God never intended for you to experience the pain that you have endured, but He can use it for good. God was with you when your heart was broken, and He wants to piece it back together again. You can say no to the lies spoken over you daily, and you can choose the truth that you are beautifully and wonderfully created by God. The Lord has an amazing plan and purpose for your life.

Wholehearted love is found only with a foundation in Jesus Christ, who covers your past, your present, and your future with His love. We hope you have begun to experience His healing power through these stories of redemption. When you find healing from your past pain or trauma, you will be ready to experience wholehearted love as God intended. Our prayer is that you can walk forward knowing His love intimately as you pursue all the dreams He has placed on your heart. You are loved beyond measure.

MAKING IT PERSONAL

Scripture to Apply

Please take some time to read the Scriptures below. Notice what they say about the key to living and loving wholeheartedly. Summarize what you see in these verses in the space provided below.

> Fear the LORD and serve him wholeheartedly. Put away forever the idols your ancestors worshiped when they lived beyond the Euphrates River and in Egypt. Serve the LORD alone. (Joshua 24:14, NLT)

> He cared for them with a true heart and led them with skillful hands. (Psalm 78:72, NLT)

Create in me a pure heart, O God, and renew a steadfast spirit within me. (Psalm 51:10)

If you look for me wholeheartedly, you will find me. (Jeremiah 29:13, NLT)

Questions to Consider

1. What does living wholeheartedly mean to you?

2. How will focusing on the qualities listed in Philippians 4:8 impact your decisions and choices as you move forward in wholehearted love?

Call to Action

Today is the day. Start now. Put the freedom cycle into action in your life. Choose to throw away the masks, stop believing the toxic thoughts, and take a stand for the truth of God in your life. As you connect with the truth over your past pain and toxic cycles, allow God to guide you as you pursue Him in a brand-new way. God has an amazing purpose and plan for you to live wholeheartedly, starting now. Claim it. You are so dearly loved, friend.

Acknowledgments

To THE WOMAN OF MY DREAMS, STEFANIE. You light up my life. Your passion for restoration over the heart of every person is contagious. We would not be writing this book if it weren't for you and your obedience to the call of God on your life. You brought hope to my life and helped restore my relationship with Jesus, and it is the greatest honor of my life to be your husband. I am forever grateful for the dreams I have been able to achieve because of you. I love working with you to help others, and it has brought me alive in purpose, hope, and wholehearted love. Most of all, I am so thankful for being able to walk out my biggest dream of being married to my best friend and the love of my life.

To the love of my life, Caleb. When we started dating in 2012, you began awakening things in my heart that I thought were dead or never knew were there. Every day since that time, you have helped me become more alive because of your love, and you continually show me a tangible example of God's love for me. I adore the man you are. You are my hero, the champion of my heart. I thank God every day for you, and it's no accident that He brought us together. It is a blessing beyond measure to serve Him together with all our hearts, to have you continually helping me become the woman God has for me to be, and to watch you fall more in love with Jesus. You are the joy of my life.

To our children, Shiloh and Asher in heaven. We long to hold you in our arms, but we know you are in safe hands. We love you, and we hope to honor you in how we help and love others. We can't wait to see you in heaven. Say hi to Jesus for us. To any future children God might bless us with: you will be our redemption story. We love you already.

To Caleb's parents, John and Kay. Your love for each other, the romance, the fun you continually cultivate show that love can last forever. Thank you for your support and encouragement in making this dream of ours come true. We feel every prayer, and we are so thankful for all the ways that you are there for us in good and difficult times. You motivate us to see the best in each other, to fight for each other, and to remember that we can all come together in prayer to have peace no matter our circumstance.

To Stefanie's parents, Ed and Susan Stack. From the time I was a little girl you believed in me to be the best I could be. You spoke so much encouragement over my creativity in writing and drawing. You have sacrificed so much for me and for the dreams God has put on my heart. I'm forever grateful for the love, sacrifice, example, and generosity you have shown me every day of my life. We are so grateful God chose you to be our parents. Your hard work ethic and the way you pour your heart and soul into loving others is such an inspiration. We don't take it for granted. We love you.

To Stefanie's grandma Maryann "Nanny" Miller, to Grandpa "Pappy" Bob Miller (now in heaven), and to Aunt Cindy. You are the most generous, loving humans. You continually think of others before yourselves. No matter what you have, you look for ways it could bless others. Pappy wrote me a letter a week for almost ten years. His funny, caring way inspired me to write and to go after my dreams. Nanny and Cindy, you continually support and love us and make this world a much better place.

To Stefanie's grandpa and grandma Bill and Tris Stack, and Aunt Dee in heaven. You continually spoke love and inspiration over me. You've taught me to trust God, and you believed in me as a writer from the time I was little and writing Christmas plays for the family. You cultivated so much fun, joy, and unconditional love.

To Caleb's grandma Marcia. Thank you for your constant and consistent love and words of encouragement. You are an inspiration for endurance and grace in my life. You have shown me how to overcome and to trust God no matter what season I am in. I am so honored to be your grandson.

To Caleb's grandma Anna and grandpa Jim in heaven. I am so grateful for the family you created and the atmosphere of hard work and perseverance that you cultivated in our family. I am forever grateful for the memories I made in Missouri with you both. I miss you so much.

To Caleb's brothers, Matt and Jesse. Thanks for loving me and supporting my dreams. You both are so dear to my heart, and I am so proud of the men that you are. Thanks for being my ride-or-die buddies. You guys are such a gift in my life. And to my sister-in-law Alicia, and our niece and nephew, Shirah and Josiah: I am so thankful for each of you, and I appreciate the love and encouragement you always show me.

To Stefanie's sister, Cristina. I'm so proud of the amazing woman and mom you are. I'm so grateful for you. It's been a blessing to get to do this life together with you since I was two. Thanks for being my little sister and being by my side through all the ups and downs. To my brother-in-law Daniel, and our nephews, Daxton and Kadan: we love you so much. You bring so much joy, laughter, and fun into our lives.

To Sarah Atkinson, Donna Berg, and the team at Tyndale

House Publishers. Thank you for believing in us, for investing in our dreams, and for helping us share our story with the world. Thank you for your intentional feedback and your kindness, and for crying with us, laughing with us, and pushing us to make this book the best it can be.

To Andrea Heinecke, Alex Field, and The Bindery Agency. Working with you has allowed us to dream bigger and make a lifelong dream become a reality. We appreciate you for believing in us and for being our advocates throughout this process.

To our endorsers. Thank you for investing the time and effort in your thoughtful and kind endorsements of our story. It means the world to us. We are honored to call you friends.

To Chelsea and Nick Hurst. Thank you for taking the time to write an amazing foreword. Your friendship and support over the years mean so much to us. We are grateful to do life with you and can't wait to continue supporting each other's dreams in the future. We love you guys.

To the friends, family, and mentors not mentioned above. You are so valued and appreciated. We couldn't have done this project without you. We see you, and we love you so much. Thank you for believing in us.

To our Cultivate Relationship and The Love Launchpad women and men, and to all those we have the huge honor of mentoring. Your courage, love, kindness, and growth are so inspiring. We love you and believe in you. We are so proud of you, and we know God is in the midst of redeeming everything in your life!

To our online community. You are loved beyond measure! God has an amazing plan for your life, and we hope this book inspires you to realize that you are not forgotten. The pain and heartbreak you have experienced are not the end of the story. God has so much in store for you! Thank you for your encouragement and support!

Notes

CHAPTER 1: WHAT'S YOUR DREAM?

1. If you would like to know more about this program, you can go to www.stefanieandcaleb.com.

CHAPTER 2: WHEN THOUGHTS TURN TOXIC

1. For some of the basic concepts about toxic thoughts in this chapter we are indebted to Dr. Terry D. Hargrave and fellow author Dr. Franz Pfitzer, and the ideas in their book *Restoration Therapy: Understanding and Guiding Healing in Marriage and Family Therapy* (New York: Routledge, 2011).
2. Hargrave and Pfitzer, 30.

CHAPTER 3: FROM COPING TO CONNECTING

1. Again, a few of the concepts in this chapter have been adapted from Terry D. Hargrave and Franz Pfitzer, *Restoration Therapy: Understanding and Guiding Healing in Marriage and Family Therapy* (New York: Routledge, 2011).
2. Dictionary.com, s.v. "coping mechanism (*n.*)," accessed January 25, 2023, https://www.dictionary.com/browse/coping-mechanism.
3. Hargrave and Pfitzer, *Restoration Therapy*, 41–42.
4. Ray Lewis, filmed May 11, 2016, at the Unexpected conference, TEDx video, 22:17, https://www.youtube.com/watch?v=DX8ZeA7ahDg.
5. Brian A. Primack et al., "Social Media Use and Perceived Social Isolation among Young Adults in the U.S.," *American Journal of Preventive Medicine* 53, no. 1 (July 2017): 1–8.
6. We are indebted to Beth Moore for this phrase about allowing God to satisfy our emptiness with His love. Beth Moore, *Breaking Free: Making Liberty in Christ a Reality in Life* (Nashville: B&H, 2000).

CHAPTER 4: STUCK IN A CYCLE
1. Some parts of our discussion of toxic cycles in this chapter are an adaptation of ideas expressed by Terry D. Hargrave and Franz Pfitzer, *Restoration Therapy: Understanding and Guiding Healing in Marriage and Family Therapy* (New York: Routledge, 2011).
2. Hargrave and Pfitzer, 43.
3. Hargrave and Pfitzer, 77.
4. *Oxford Dictionary of English* (Oxford: Oxford University Press, 2010), s.v. "responsibility."

CHAPTER 5: IS GOD REALLY GOOD?
1. *Merriam-Webster*, s.v. "violate (*v.*)," accessed February 12, 2023, https://www.merriam-webster.com/dictionary/violate.

CHAPTER 6: AT THE END OF YOUR ROPE
1. C. S. Lewis, *The Four Loves* (San Francisco: HarperOne, 2017), 155–156.
2. "Whole Heart (Hold Me Now)," by Joel Timothy Houston and Aodhan Thomas King, track 4 on Hillsong UNITED, *People*, Hillsong Music and Resources, 2019.
3. *Concise Oxford American Dictionary* (Oxford: Oxford University Press, 2006), s.v. "surrender."

CHAPTER 7: THE TRUTH SETS US FREE
1. "Praise You in This Storm," by Bernie Herms and John Mark Hall, track 2 on Casting Crowns, *Lifesong*, Beach Street Records, 2005.

CHAPTER 8: ACTING IN TRUTH
1. Many of the items on this list are adapted from themes covered in Terry D. Hargrave and Franz Pfitzer, *Restoration Therapy: Understanding and Guiding Healing in Marriage and Family Therapy* (New York: Routledge, 2011), 38, 188.
2. "When I Say I Do," by Matthew West, track 2 on *Hold You Up*, Sparrow Records, 2010.

CHAPTER 9: THE FREEDOM CYCLE
1. The freedom cycle is partially derived from the "pain-and-peace cycle" in Terry D. Hargrave and Franz Pfitzer, *Restoration Therapy: Understanding and Guiding Healing in Marriage and Family Therapy* (New York: Routledge, 2011).
2. Hargrave and Pfitzer, 188.
3. For more about the "love languages," see Gary Chapman, *The Five Love*

Languages: How to Express Heartfelt Commitment to Your Mate (Chicago: Moody, 2009), ebook, especially chapters 4–8.

4. Henry Cloud, *Changes That Heal: Four Practical Steps to a Happier, Healthier You* (Grand Rapids, MI: Zondervan, 2018), 142.

5. Martin Luther King Jr., *Strength to Love* (Boston: Beacon Press, 2019), 47.

CHAPTER 10: SEEN, KNOWN, LOVED

1. Encyclopedia.com, s.v. "noble (*adj.*)," updated June 11, 2018, https://www.encyclopedia.com/noble.

2. Encyclopedia.com, s.v. "right (*adj.*)," updated May 11, 2018, https://www.encyclopedia.com/social-sciences-and-law/political-science-and-government/political-science-terms-and-concepts/right.

About The Authors

CALEB AND STEFANIE ROUSE consider themselves "modern missionaries" working full-time together to help others have amazing relationships. They are counselors, digital creators, and authors. They are dedicated to helping people in all stages attain a positive relationship with God, others, and themselves so that they can be empowered to act in love, selflessness, and self-control and as a result, have successful and meaningful relationships. Stefanie and Caleb speak daily to a broad audience across their social media platforms about faith and relationships. Known for their authenticity and vulnerability, they share stories of hope, loss, and love that inspire people from all around the globe.

Before starting their online ministry, Stefanie and Caleb were teachers together at a private Christian school in Southern California. Stefanie taught classes on relationships and biblical studies after having served as a full-time counselor, and Caleb taught AP World History. Stefanie holds a master's degree in marriage and family therapy with an emphasis in theology from Fuller Theological Seminary, and Caleb has his master's degree in education from Azusa Pacific University. They have applied their education and counseling skills to the creation of a signature online course called Cultivate Relationship, through which they serve their community of singles and married couples. Stefanie and Caleb counsel and work with people from all over the world. They have seen significant breakthroughs in the lives of their clients, who have gone from brokenhearted to happily married. They are passionate about seeing single people set up for a firm foundation in their current season of life. Their desire is for them to walk out each day living life abundantly, hopefully, and authentically as they feel safe in The Love Launchpad Community that Caleb and Stefanie created.

In 2021, the Rouses published their first book, *A Year of Prayer: Daily Moments of Contemplation, Devotion & Grace.* They have been featured in news outlets across the world for their viral content on social media, and they have made podcast appearances together and separately on topics related to faith and relationships.

Before their current pursuits, the couple spent a few years as photographers and lifestyle and travel bloggers. They loved being hired by cities and top hotels all over the country and internationally. Known for their beautiful photography and authentic voice, they shared their experiences and activities as they explored breathtaking locations.

Stefanie and Caleb currently reside in Pittsburgh, PA. They have two babies in heaven named Asher and Shiloh, and they share their home with their fur baby, a Pomeranian named Honey Bear. Caleb and Stefanie enjoy spending as much time together as possible participating in their hobbies of hiking, outdoor activities, exploring new cities and countries, playing board games, or watching their favorite shows.

Contact the Rouses at stefanieandcaleb.com or PO Box 378, Bradford Woods, PA 15015. Follow them on Instagram (@stefanie.rouse, @calebjasonrouse), on TikTok (@stefanieandcaleb), and on YouTube (@stefanieandcaleb).